STRANGE WORLDS, FANTASTIC PLACES

THE EARTH, ITS WONDERS, ITS SECRETS

STRANGE WORLDS, FANTASTIC PLACES

Reader's Digest

PUBLISHED BY

THE READER'S DIGEST ASSOCIATION LIMITED

LONDON NEW YORK MONTREAL SYDNEY CAPE TOWN

STRANGE WORLDS, FANTASTIC PLACES
Edited and designed by Toucan Books Limited, London,
for the Reader's Digest Association Limited, London
Written by Antony Mason
Edited by Jane MacAndrew and Andrew Kerr-Jarrett
Designed by Bob Burroughs, Bradbury and Williams
Picture research by Elizabeth Walsh

FOR THE READER'S DIGEST
Series Editor Christine Noble
Editorial Assistant Alison Candlin

READER'S DIGEST GENERAL BOOKS
Editor Kathryn Bonomi
Art Editor Eleanor Kostyk
Research Assistants Mary Jo McLean, Valerie Sylvester
The photo credits that appear on page 160 are hereby made a part
of this copyright page.

Printed in the United States of America
1998

Library of Congress Cataloging in Publication Data
Strange worlds, fantastic places / [edited by Jane MacAndrew and
    Andrew Kerr-Jarrett].
            p.   cm.—(The earth, its wonders, its secrets)
        Includes index.
        ISBN 0-7621-0071-0
        1. Natural areas. 2. Natural history. 3. Ecology.
    I. MacAndrew, Jane. II. Kerr-Jarrett, Andrew. III. Reader's
    Digest Association. IV. Series.
    QH75; S6738   1997
    508—dc21   97-38045

FRONT COVER *The red-brown pinnacles and buttresses of Bryce Canyon
in Utah have been shaped by erosion over millions of years.
Inset: Chinstrap penguins congregate on a melting iceberg in the Antarctic.*

PAGE 3 *The permafrost of the Siberian tundra lies beneath a soggy mat
of soil, grass, moss, and lichen. Reindeer live and die amid this vast landscape, where once mammoths roamed.*

CONTENTS

ADAPTING TO EXTREMES

Cast away among clouds on a remote tropical mountaintop, at the heart of a searing desert, on far-flung coral atolls and deep within the Earth, lie strange and fantastic worlds that are inhabited by some of nature's most adaptable species.

In the dense jungles of the eastern part of the Democratic Republic of Congo (formerly known as Zaire), dizzying snow-capped peaks tower over the sweltering tropical lowlands. Glaciers sparkle and groan in the bright, thin air. These are the Virunga Range and the Ruwenzori Mountains – soaring massifs that have been identified as the 'Mountains of the Moon', legendary source of the River Nile. This at least was the name they bore on a map of what was then the known world

attributed to the Greek-Egyptian astronomer Ptolemy. He worked in the great library of Alexandria in the early 2nd century AD.

For the next 1600 years geographers and explorers remained in the dark about the true source of the River Nile, and in the late 19th century it seemed for a while that

the ancient Greeks had been right all along. Certainly, some of the waters that feed Lake Albert, across which the Nile flows near the start of its long journey from Lake Victoria in the East African highlands to the Mediterranean, have their source in the Ruwenzori Mountains.

ALIEN WORLD *Groundsels cut tousle-headed silhouettes high in the Ruwenzori Mountains of the Democratic Republic of Congo.*

RARE GEMS *Palm trees cluster around the life-giving water of a Moroccan oasis – an island of life in a sea of aridity.*

The Greeks' haunting name for these mountains suggests direct experience of them, for the higher one climbs towards the peaks, the more other-worldly they become. Between 15 000 ft (4572 m) and 20 000 ft (6096 m), just beneath the snow-line, lies a landscape that might belong to science fiction. Giant groundsels – outlandish relatives of Europe's dainty yellow-flowered hedgerow plant – grow to more than 20 ft (6 m) high. Close by, and in vivid contrast to their ungainly cabbage heads, grow equally extravagant giant lobelia, topped by a headdress of silvery leaves.

Snugly insulated against the cold by their furry leaves and blankets of dead foliage, these giants are uniquely adapted to their environment. Any higher, and they would be killed by the chill, and unable to draw nutrients from the frozen soil. Any lower, and their bulk would draw the fatal fire of the tropical heat. They exist only in their own highly specialised niche of the Earth's many and varied habitats – a narrow, equatorial slice of the globe's altitudes.

ECOLOGICAL ISLANDS

There are many such places in the world, where accidents of geology, climate and time have created extraordinary landscapes and unique environments, and where plants and animals have had to adapt and evolve to match the conditions – in caves, deserts, polar regions, the shallows of tropical seas.

Small, remote islands, bounded by vast areas of sea, can provide the kind of isolation that best demonstrates the evolutionary process at work – as Charles Darwin, the pioneer of evolutionary theory, discovered on the Galápagos Islands when he visited them in the 1830s. But it is not just the sea that isolates. There are plenty of other 'islands' of life, cut off from the neighbouring worlds, where unique species, or unique combinations of species, have developed. Oases, for example, clustering around rare supplies of water in the desert, are often referred to as 'islands of green'. Rising high above the tropical forests of southern Venezuela are

TIDAL HAVEN *A starfish shares a tide pool with other creatures thrown together by the waves on Canada's Pacific shore.*

the *tepuís* – huge table-top outcrops with such sheer sides that many of the summits have never been visited. The flat tops – strange islands among the rain clouds – are dotted with plants found nowhere else on Earth.

Climate and altitude can similarly create unique ecological zones. The high equatorial landscape of Ruwenzori and Virunga, with its giant groundsel and giant lobelia, is isolated by the unique climatic conditions which exist at that altitude. The conditions above and below are every bit as much a barrier as the girdle of water around an island.

ON A SCALE WITH MILLIONS
Enormous herds of caribou range across the tundra of Canada and Alaska.

Tidal wetlands occupy the margin between sea and dry land. These areas are shaped by the effects of another dimension, one that leaves its mark on all types of environments: time. To the ever-ticking clock of the tides, the landscape is utterly transformed twice a day, as the different animals of high and low tide alternate their shifts.

WORLDS OF THEIR OWN

The majority of these strange worlds are, almost by definition, remote places. If access to them were too easy, then their genetic pool would be constantly replenished from the wider world and there would be little to set them apart. Because they are remote – or have been until the recent past – they seem unfamiliar, full of surprises. They are isolated worlds, each with their own food chain and their own strategies for survival.

Some depend on microclimates – small, sometimes miniature zones which buck the trend of the surrounding climate. Towering pinnacles of rock, low scoops of land in a plain, burrows beneath the desert sands, hot volcanic vents in the depths of the ocean, rocks that catch the sun in the polar wastes – each may offer some small but significant environmental advantage that enables it to support its own distinct chain of life.

The conditions that form such an environment, and the life forms that interact within it, represent an immensely complex web of relationships – summarised by the term 'ecosystem'. Tiny ecosystems, as in Antarctica, can consist of a patch of moss and the insects and bacteria that live within it. Others are unique environments on a grand scale, where the conditions are consistent enough to categorise them as a distinctive ecosystem – such as the grassland steppes of Central Asia; or coastal deserts, where plants and animals survive on condensed droplets of fog; or the tundra, home to migrating caribou and billions of mosquitoes. Ultimately, however, all ecosystems are interconnected. The entire world is an ecosystem.

ON THE EDGE *A dead tree rises from the Namib Desert where most moisture comes from droplets of water carried by coastal fogs.*

WHERE THERE'S WATER
*The extensive root system of the
white gum enables it to thrive in
Western Australia's arid
Hamersley Range.*

PATTERNS IN SPACE
*Competition for light and water
results in airy canopies of
eucalyptus trees, growing in a
forest in South Australia.*

Many of the relationships within an ecosystem simply express the links in the food chain. The lions of the Ngorongoro crater feed off herbivores such as gazelles, waterbuffalo and zebras, which breed sufficiently quickly to tolerate the loss. But other relationships involve more complex interdependencies – or ingenious arrangements of give-and-take.

Living among the gum trees that line the creeks of inland Australia, ants offer protection to the caterpillar of the genoveva azure butterfly as it makes its nightly journey to the top of the tree to feed on mistletoe. In return, the ants milk the sweet honeydew secreted by the caterpillar while it passes the day in their underground nests. In the coral reefs off Aldabra, a remote island in the Seychelles group in the western Indian Ocean, the small cleaner wrasse is allowed to feed in the mouth of some much bigger fish, such as a large sweetlips. Tolerated by the bigger fish, the wrasse delicately picks off bacteria that might otherwise infect wounds inflicted by the sweetlip's habit of grazing among sharp coral.

THE LIMITS OF SCIENCE

Every year, huge volumes of carefully gathered information add to our understanding of the intricate mechanisms of ecosystems, and the habits of the plants and animals within them.

Today, there are scientific explanations for phenomena that, just decades ago, were baffling mysteries or even unthought of. The more people learn – for example, about the creatures of the ocean deeps, or about the ability of bacteria to remain dormant over thousands of years – the more complex the web of life appears. Yet increasingly it becomes possible to argue the case for the interconnectedness of all things.

Many of the larger questions can be answered only by theory. Even evolution, after all, is still no more than a theory and – although at present it appears to many to

SHAPED BY SURROUNDINGS
A pinyon pine has found its special niche, clinging to a rocky crest in Utah's Escalante Canyon (right). Other trees (below) have found niches along the seasonal watercourses of Arizona's Canyon de Chelly.

FAIR EXCHANGE *An Oriental sweetlips hovers patiently as a cleaner wrasse picks bacteria from its body – food given in return for a useful service.*

Human knowledge about the world may be great enough to fill libraries with detailed and learned publications – yet is all this merely a scratch on the surface? In fact, the surface of the globe has now been extensively mapped – but much of the finer detail remains to be filled in. If the earth were a peach, with the atmosphere the bloom on the peach, the mapped and surveyed portion of the world would be no deeper than the peach skin. If, even in the 1990s, it is still possible to discover entire tribes in the Amazon rain forest who have never before been contacted by the outside world, how many species of microscopic animals are left for scientists to identify? And virtually nothing is known about what lies beneath the surface of the Earth.

Ignorance invites wonder: knowledge reveals the huge scale of our ignorance. Science can help to explain the strange and fantastic worlds of remote wildernesses and isolated ecosystems – but it cannot hope to supplant their sense of mystery, or dispel our wonder at the flexible, multifaceted powers of nature which have shaped them.

LIFE AT THE MARGINS
Seaweed clings to rocks on the California coast. Only a few species can stand the buffeting in such intertidal zones.

be the best explanation there is for the way that life forms alter over time, and how human beings have arrived where they are – every aspect of the theory is still fiercely debated by scientists. Evolution is an attempt to explain how – but does not explain why, and provides no template for the future besides speculation.

SECRET WORLDS

1

SUMMIT CASCADES *Waterfalls plunge down the sheer rock faces of Venezuelan* tepuís.

JUST AS THE EARTH ITSELF IS AN ISLAND OF LIFE SET AMID THE SEEMING DESERT OF THE REST OF THE KNOWN UNIVERSE, SO THERE ARE SMALL POCKETS ON OUR PLANET WHICH ARE MARKEDLY DIFFERENT FROM THE WORLD AROUND — MICROCOSMS WITHIN THE WHOLE. ISOLATED BY IMPENETRABLE TERRAIN OR BY WATER, OR SIMPLY HIDDEN FROM VIEW, THEY PROVIDE A UNIQUE SET OF CONDITIONS IN WHICH TO NURTURE THEIR OWN SPECIALLY ADAPTED PLANTS AND ANIMALS. THESE INWARD-LOOKING, SELF-DEFINING PLACES — SECRET VALLEYS, DARK CAVES, PRISTINE TROPICAL ISLANDS FRINGED WITH PURE WHITE SAND — REVERBERATE WITH A STRONG SENSE OF INDIVIDUALITY AND MYSTIQUE.

SLOW MOTION *A giant tortoise on the Galápagos Islands.*

LOST WORLDS

Many isolated places have evolved unique ecosystems. The table-top mountains of Venezuela, known as tepuís, *are so remote that they inspired Sir Arthur Conan Doyle to fantasise that dinosaurs might have survived there into modern times.*

Only in the era of the helicopter and advanced climbing gear have the summits of the *tepuís* in the Guiana Highlands of southern Venezuela become widely accessible. Even then, conditions are often atrocious, with thick, rain-laden clouds veiling the summits and frequent electrical storms bouncing around the deep chasms. Over 60 in (150 cm) of rain falls every year and after a rainstorm the runoff from the high plateaus surges down into the rivers below, sometimes raising the water level by 20 ft (6 m) in a matter of minutes.

Tepuí is, simply, the word for 'mountain' in the language of the Pemón Indians who live in the region – but so unusual are these mountains that the Indian word has been adopted to describe them. They stretch out over an area of more than 200 000 sq miles (518 000 km²), although the main cluster around Mount Roraima covers just 15 000 sq miles (38 850 km²). From a sweltering rain forest – a lush green carpet of foliage inhabited by parrots, monkeys, and swarms of mosquitoes – the *tepuís* rise 5000 ft (1524 m) or more in sheer, rugged cliffs to their flat table tops. At the foot there may be angled shelves called *talus*, where profuse foliage grows, but the escarpments themselves are often too unstable and sheer even for tenacious rainforest plants to take hold. The majority of the

HEADS IN THE CLOUDS *The* **tepuís'** *table-top summits tower over the forests at their feet.*

summits are completely cut off from the world below.

This region was once pinpointed as a possible location for El Dorado, the fabled city of gold which lured Spanish conquistadores ever deeper into the jungles of South America. In the mid 19th century, gold was indeed found in the rivers of the Guiana Highlands, encouraging prospectors to brave this unforgiving climate and landscape, where they built shanty towns at El Callao and the optimistically named El Dorado.

Only the most determined travellers ventured farther south. They included Richard Schomburgk, a German botanist, who, in 1842 dubbed the region a 'botanical El Dorado'. In 1884 the botanist Everard Im Thurn explored the region on behalf of the British Royal Geographical Society. He climbed Mount Roraima, at 9094 ft (2772 m) the highest *tepuí*, and returned with plants that had never been seen before. A lecture about this expedition proved to be a long-term inspiration for the young Arthur Conan Doyle, creator of Sherlock Holmes. It sowed the seeds of an idea which emerged in 1912 as *The Lost World* – the first of his Professor Challenger stories, in which the professor travels to a remote and mysterious land where dinosaurs have survived.

ISLANDS IN THE CLOUDS

Thin waterfalls drift in the wind like streamers from the crests of the *tepuí* summits. Among them is the world's highest waterfall, Angel Falls, which cascades 3212 ft (979 m) down a sheer escarpment from the rim of Auyan Tepuí. From below, this seems a miraculous feat: how can all that water emerge from a point so close to the summit? The answer is clear from the air: the

BIG DROP *The Angel Falls, the world's highest, spill from the lip of Auyan Tepuí.*

THE ANGEL OF THE FALLS

It would be an understandable mistake to think that the world's highest waterfall was named after celestial beings. In fact it takes its name from the man who first brought news of the falls to the outside world, an American pilot and adventurer named Jimmy Angel (1899-1956).

Jimmy Angel was a larger-than-life flying ace, who served underage in the Royal Canadian Flying Corps during the First World War, set several flying records, and performed as a stunt pilot for films. In 1921 he met a gold prospector in Panama who told him of a river yielding vast quantities of gold in the El Dorado region of southern Venezuela. Angel flew to Venezuela with this prospector and, true enough, the expedition yielded considerable quantities of gold. Later, Angel attempted in vain to locate this river again from the air, and it became something of an obsession. On one of his missions in 1935 he came across the towering falls of Auyan Tepuí. Fascinated by this discovery, he persuaded a Venezuelan explorer to join him and his wife on a trip to investigate the falls. The plan was to land on the summit of Auyan Tepuí, but what he thought was solid flat ground turned out to be bog and his plane was marooned. The three then had to find their way off the summit, a journey that took two gruelling weeks – by which time they had been given up for dead.

Angel Falls was officially confirmed as the highest waterfall in the world in 1949. Six years later, in 1956, Jimmy Angel was killed in a plane crash in Panama. His ashes were scattered over Angel Falls, whose name remains his lasting memorial.

DEFYING LABELS *Jimmy Angel was as restless as the falls named after him.*

THE TEPUÍS: ANCIENT REMNANTS OF A LOST CONTINENT

The *tepuís* represent the surviving bastions of harder rock in a vast sandstone plateau which has been eroded over hundreds of millions of years. Once, perhaps 2 billion years ago, a combination of wind and water deposited a thick layer of sand on top of a shield of harder metamorphic rock. This upper layer later fused into sandstone and formed a plateau in the great ancient continent of Gondwanaland. Around 180 million years ago Gondwanaland split apart, forming Africa and South America. The immense pressures exerted in this process fractured the plateau to create vertical fissures that would later become the cliff walls.

Millions of years of weathering have etched away much of this sandstone plateau down to the metamorphic rock – leaving the sheer, toothy outcrops of harder rock, with flat tops showing where once the plateau had been. The *tepuís* rise to about 5000 ft (1524 m) on average, while the highest, Mount Roraima, stands at 9094 ft (2772 m), pushed upwards by the movement of the tectonic plates. The process was complete by some 4 million years ago, when the *tepuís* began to look more or less as they do today.

The summits may appear flat from a distance, but this is an illusion. Some parts are thickly forested, some are pitted with treacherous hollows or impenetrable bogs, while others are coated with hostile ranks of sharp, contorted rocks, fashioned into pillars and arches. Black and seemingly lifeless, the bare rocks resemble fields of volcanic lava, but are in fact eroded sandstone coated with black algae. The effect is even more astonishing on Mount Roraima, where the blackened surfaces contrast with areas of glistening pink and white quartzite – the natural colour of the sandstone.

BURSTING FROM THE SEAMS *Vegetation sprouts from gaps between the algae-blackened rocks that line the jagged summit of Mount Roraima.*

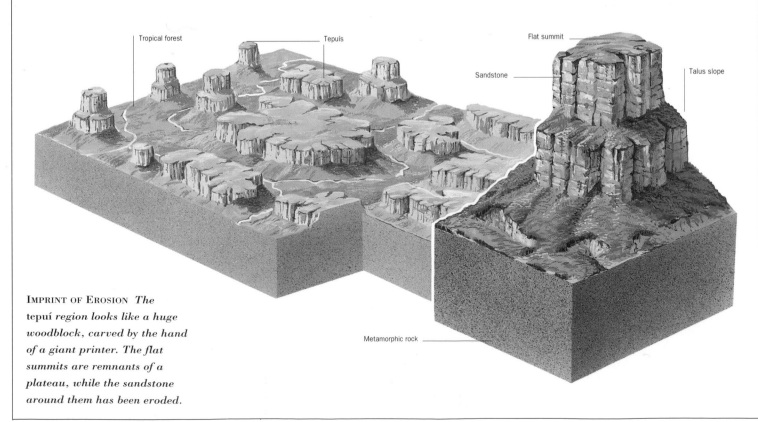

Tropical forest

Tepuís

Flat summit

Sandstone

Talus slope

Metamorphic rock

IMPRINT OF EROSION *The tepuí region looks like a huge woodblock, carved by the hand of a giant printer. The flat summits are remnants of a plateau, while the sandstone around them has been eroded.*

flat top of Auyan Tepuí is a 300 sq mile (777 km²) plateau, a massive catchment area for the rains. The flow of Angel Falls and similar waterfalls varies considerably. The big rains of the summer months send vast quantities of water gushing down the precipices. But in other seasons many of the waterfalls fade into ribbon-like trickles, and some become so wispy that the water never reaches the foot of the cliff. It turns

QUEST FOR EL DORADO

When Spanish conquistadores discovered gold in Central and South America in the early 16th century, it excited an all-consuming passion for treasure, and the legend of the kingdom of El Dorado – the gilded man – was born. The quest for El Dorado took the conquistadores ever farther beyond their new territories, into the southern part of what is now the USA and into the Amazon jungles. In fact, little gold was found in the Amazon until the 1850s. Then a minor gold rush ensued in southern Venezuela, inspired by the discovery of a nugget weighing 15 lb (6.8 kg). Some 8000 settlers poured in. By the 1880s the region was yielding 15 tons a year. The fever abated as finds dwindled, but aircraft later took prospectors such as Jimmy Angel deeper into the highlands. Even today a few adventurers roam this untamed land, trying their luck.

first into a thin spray, then a mist, and then vaporises in the heat of the rain forest below.

The summits of the *tepuís* are 10°C (18°F) cooler than the rain forest – but it is not just the temperature that makes them a world apart. In contrast to the dense jungle below, many of the summits present unaccommodating worlds of flat stone pavements and jumbles of jagged, weathered rock which are so frequently awash with rain that they are bare of soil. Instead, lichens and mosses – clinging to tiny fissures in the rock – provide isolated rafts to which larger plants,

such as bromeliads, cling for life. Elsewhere, rocky hollows are filled with dense jungles, where tangles of bromeliads and orchids grow out of heaps of decaying debris.

Each *tepuí* is a world of its own, with a unique set of conditions to which plant life

has had to adapt. Some 10 000 plant species have been found on the summits, of which about half are found nowhere else, including five kinds of carnivorous marsh pitcher plants – living on five separate *tepuís*. By catching insects and absorbing their dissolved

WARTS AND ALL *The Roraima toad merges into the wet, blackened rocks of the* tepuís.

pink lupins and yellow marguerites after the rains, and golden-brown as the dry season burnishes the thick carpet of long grasses.

The sheer scale of the crater is impressive. This vast caldera – the sixth largest in the world – was formed by the collapse of the heart of a volcano more than 2 million years ago. It now stands at 5600ft (1706m) above sea level and measures 11 miles (18 km) across, with walls rising steeply some 2000ft (610m) to the ragged crest of the rim. It is a massive amphitheatre, dappled with patches of acacia forest, cloud shadow and the ever-changing colours of the passing hours.

bodies, these plants are able to survive in a world deprived of nutrients by the constant wash of the rains. Other carnivorous plants on the *tepuís* include sparkling sundews, with their brilliant flowers that attract insects to the fatal pool of nectar. Bladderworts survive with no roots at all. They float in the water and use hollow bladders as a trap to catch tiny water organisms, which they are able to dissolve and digest within two hours.

Animal life on the *tepuís* has proved more disappointing. Pumas live on them, and scarlet macaws roost on their ledges, feeding in the forests below. The only unique creature found on them is a kind of toad, whose dark, warty skin provides good camouflage among the blackened, rain-slaked rocks. So far, though, no dinosaurs.

NOAH'S ARK IN A CRATER

Elsewhere in the world the combination of physical isolation and climate has brought very different results. High above the plains of northern Tanzania, the huge ancient volcanic crater of Ngorongoro is raised towards the African skies like a sacred, jewelled chalice. Its inside is emerald green studded with

THE COMFORT OF PLENTY
Wildebeest rest from their grazing in the Ngorongoro crater's lush spring meadows.

IN THE PINK *Flamingos flock to the mineral-rich lakes on the floor of the Ngorongoro crater (left). Masai herders stand with their cattle (above).*

NATURE IN THE RAW

The Ngorongoro crater rings an enclosed world of great beauty – beauty which is at once both majestic and savage. The pressure of the food chain is intense, and every link within it has to be perpetually on guard. A wildebeest caught grazing away from the herd – or slowed by illness, injury or the presence of young – will soon be singled out by hyenas, or lions.

The lions hold the undisputed position as the top carnivores, fulfilling their need to eat over 10 lb (4.5 kg) of meat per day. There are some 80 lions in the crater, divided into about ten prides. Almost all of these lions were born in the crater – for the steep caldera walls and availability of food throughout the year ensure that there is not much movement between the crater and the world beyond. Indeed, some observers fear the danger of in-breeding.

The lionesses do the bulk of the hunting, well camouflaged in the grasses during the dry season when the pickings are thinner on the ground. They go about it with ruthless efficiency, working as a team to harry, weaken and kill the larger grazers, such as the water buffalo. Even so, their success rate is comparatively low: only about a third of their attempted strikes are successful.

When sure of killing a selected buffalo, the lionesses will take turns to mount it and gnaw at its back, safely out of range of its hefty horns. Exhausted and despairing, the buffalo will collapse and the lionesses begin feasting, regardless of whether their prey is still alive or not.

The lions are not immune from attack. Isolated cubs may be picked off by hyenas or groups of wildebeest and buffalo. Even adult lionesses, outwitted in the hunt, can be surrounded, wounded and trampled to death by buffalo. There is no such thing as dying peacefully of old age: virtually all life here ends violently, when an animal no longer has the strength to defend itself against the brutal pressures of the food chain.

ON THE PROWL *Lionesses stroll across open ground in the Ngorongoro crater.*

Spread across its floor is one of the richest concentrations of wildlife in Africa: elephants, lions, cheetahs, leopards, jackals, hyenas, zebra, water buffalo, wildebeest, black rhinoceroses, hippopotamuses, gazelles, warthogs, baboons, ostriches, vultures, egrets, herons, marabou storks, red billed oxpeckers, flamingos and many more. The crater is now protected as a conservation area. It was once home to Masai communities, who are now permitted to remain in the crater only while tending their herds of cattle.

The birds of the crater are largely transitory guests, attracted to its floor by soda lakes rich in sodium carbonate washed in from the surrounding volcanic soil. They create patches of deep blue that reflect the sky, except when millions of flamingos congregate, enhancing the crater's colour with their haze of pink. A permanent if variable water supply, from two rivers, and the lakes and swamps, supports so much life in the Ngorongoro crater.

Each year, at the onset of the dry season, the larger animals of the Serengeti plain below set off on migrations in search of water and new pasture. In contrast, most of their counterparts in Ngorongoro stay in the crater throughout the year – although some will wend their way in and out of the crater each year along centuries-old animal trails.

With the annual 'long rains' of January and February, the grass springs back to life in the richly fertile volcanic soil, supporting thousands of grazers and all the attendant carnivores. Because of its rich and permanent population of animals, Ngorongoro has frequently been referred to as a kind of 'Noah's Ark' – where the timeless rhythms and life cycles of so many East African species, and the highly charged interrelationships between them, are played out within the boundaries of its enclosing walls.

NATURAL REFUGE

The safety of isolation can also be found in places where the landscape is simply too difficult to cross. The Ankarana Plateau of northern Madagascar consists of karst limestone – a brittle landscape pitted with hollows and caves. In places the limestone has been weathered by the heavy rainfall,

70 in (1778 mm) per annum, into needle-like spikes. Some are 100 ft (30 m) tall, while others form closely packed ranks of needles. This weathered limestone is capable of carving up a good pair of shoes and will lacerate the paws of any unwary animal.

It is known locally as *tsingy* – an imitation of the ringing sound the stone makes when tapped. Like the clusters of spikes that used

MADAGASCAN RAMPARTS *Limestone pinnacles in the tsingy lands (below) provide natural defences for species such as the shy nocturnal aye-aye (left).*

to protect forts from cavalry, the *tsingy* lands help to protect the refuges of many of Madagascar's unique animal species. These include the lemurs, a branch of primates distantly related to monkeys, which live in trees growing from fissures in the limestone. Tiny dwarf lemurs, ringtailed lemurs, crowned lemurs, sifakas and indris – the largest and noisiest of the family – are all found on the plateau. Their name comes from the Latin *lemures*, meaning 'a ghost', a reference to their largely nocturnal lifestyle. Of all of them, the cat-sized aye-aye is probably the best adapted to nocturnal life. It has huge ears and an acute sense of smell. By tapping

MADAGASCAN TERROR

Unlike Africa, Madagascar has no large mammal predators – but the fossa, though small, can be very dangerous. This vicious carnivore looks superficially like a kind of short-legged, flat-footed puma, but is in fact a member of the viverrine family, which includes mongooses and civets. It generally lives in trees, including those on the Ankarana plateau. Using their hooked claws, fossas hunt birds and small mammals, but on occasion breeding groups will tackle much larger prey, such as oxen and even, according to local legend, humans. They are skilled climbers, and will pursue agile lemurs into the treetops. Fossas, like civets, emit a foul-smelling secretion when cornered.

on the branches and trunks of dead trees, it locates the presence of the larvae of wood-boring beetles, then winkles them out using a very long, specially adapted middle finger.

The plateau's other unusual inhabitants include the tenrec, a shrew-like animal that feeds off grubs and worms; large crocodiles, measuring up to 20 ft (6 m) which, unusually, retreat into the caves during the dry season and drift into sleepy repose; and the aggressive carnivore, the fossa.

KILLER INSTINCT *The fossa is the most ferocious meat-eating mammal of Madagascar's Ankarana plateau.*

HIDDEN VALLEYS

The power of water can scour deep paths through rock. In remote areas, where the sides of gorges and canyons are steep and deep, small isolated worlds may develop, fed by the river water and sheltered from the extremes of weather.

The Elburz Mountains in northern Iran rise to a series of craggy peaks, some over 18 000 ft (5500 m) above sea level. The sunlight that pours down through the thin air is intensely bright, lighting up a landscape of barren rock and scree slopes, which fade away in layer upon layer of delicate pastel shades – ochre, burnt sienna, umber, rose – into the mauve distance. It is a parched land, yet the mountains rise high enough for snow to fall on the upper slopes even in summer and the highest peaks are snow-capped throughout the year. Water drains from the snowy heights, and bubbles forth from springs lower down, filling the winding valleys with fast-flowing streams and rivers.

From high up, these river valleys present a remarkable sight. Running through the dust-dry surrounding slopes are narrow ribbons of intense green. Everywhere along the

THE GIFT OF WATER *High in Iran's Elburz Mountains (left), rivers bring life to the soil on their banks. In the Samariá Gorge of Crete (below) water has carved out a superb refuge.*

valley – everywhere within reach of the water, and where plants can find purchase for their roots – there is rich, abundant and healthy life. Paths lead through pastures, orchards and shady stands of poplars. Villagers, living in clusters of mud-brick houses, extend the area of fertile land by means of irrigation channels, watering fields where they grow wheat, onions, lettuce and eggplants.

Humans have long used hidden valleys as refuges where the natural defence provided by their walls is complemented by the

HOME OF THE ASSASSINS

The Alamut Valley in the Elburz Mountains was once headquarters to a Shiite Islamic sect. Under Hasan i Sabbah (d 1124), it gained control of a swathe of territory using a special technique. Sect members infiltrated the courts of rival powers, and assassinated key players. It is said that Hasan i Sabbah won his followers' loyalty by administering hashish to them to create an impression of the paradise they would enjoy after death. The sect members were called *hahshashin* – 'eaters of hashish' – from which the English 'assassin' is derived.

presence of water and the fertility that goes with it. For centuries, the Samariá Gorge in Crete provided a safe haven for refugees from vendettas. Plants and animals also flourish in this environment, which is noticeably greener than the rocky slopes of the surrounding Levká Ori (White Mountains). The valley floor, above the annual flood level, and the steep walls of the gorge are dotted with tough grasses, and shrubs and trees such as oleanders, figs and cypresses, which create sufficient food sources for a range of mammals from mice to wild goats, and attract the birds of prey that feed off them.

CANYON LANDS

Some rivers produce even more dramatic havens. The Escalante River Canyon, surrounded by the desert of southern Utah, contains intimate pockets of life among the barren rock. Sunlight falling through cavernous bowls of rock alights upon patches of damp soil on the river bank, drawing out carpets of green where grass and wild asters grow, attracting migrant mallard ducks to the pools of slack water at the river's edge.

The Escalante River now flows into Lake Powell, an artificial lake on the Colorado River, which then flows on into the supreme hidden valley: the Grand Canyon. The statistics of the Grand Canyon are astonishing. Averaging 1 mile (1.6 km) deep and 9 miles (15 km) wide, it runs for 280 miles (450 km). The rock strata that line its walls represent

GREEN FLASH *Green trees and bushes mark the winding path of the Escalante River in Utah.*

a record of some 2 billion years of geological history. Oddly, though, the river has flowed at about the same height above sea level for 5 million years. It is the surrounding landscape that has been pushed upwards over the millennia, but slowly enough for the river to scrape out its path through the rising strata of rock at each successive phase.

PIONEER OF THE GRAND CANYON

They thought he was mad to take such risks – but John Wesley Powell (1834-1902) was not easily dissuaded. This professor of natural sciences from Illinois, who had lost his right forearm in the American Civil War, was determined to forge a path along one of the great unknowns of the West, the mighty Grand Canyon. He set out in May 1869 from the railhead at Green River, Wyoming, with four specially built open boats and nine men, well planned supplies and carefully packed scientific equipment. They first steered their way down the Green River, often hauling the boats overland to skirt around impassable rocks and cataracts. At 'Disaster Falls' they lost a boat and a third of their provisions, and one man deserted. In August they eventually reached the Colorado river and begun the real journey, plunging down the rapids, learning as they went. It was an exhausting and frightening experience, and the men, bothered by mosquitoes, dwindling food rations and Powell's unswerving determination, came close to mutiny.

Eventually three of the team – all professional trappers – despaired and deserted. They made their way up the canyon walls and were never seen again: it later transpired that they were ambushed and killed by Havasupai Indians. Ironically they had deserted at the very end of the journey – for, just two days later, Powell and his remaining crew of five emerged triumphant at the western end of the canyon.

Powell became a celebrated hero, but he did not rest on his laurels.

He mounted a much larger expedition to the region in 1871-2, and in the remaining three decades of his life he fought vigorously for the issues that concerned him. He was a founder of the US Geological Survey, which today continues the detailed mapping service and resource analysis which he initiated. Powell was also one of the founders of the National Geographical Society. He was a friend of the Indians, notably the Paiute, and sympathised with their plight. Foreseeing the dangers which their loss of culture presented, he lobbied for the creation of the Bureau of American Ethnology. He warned against unregulated settlement of the West and campaigned for a federal policy towards water management and damming. Here his pleas went largely unheard, resulting in the overuse of land and a series of disastrous crop failures and dustbowls in the 1890s and 1930s. In 1963, as part of the great federal programme to improve water distribution and management in the West, the Colorado was dammed at Glen Canyon and, fittingly, the new lake was named Lake Powell.

OUT WEST *Powell (standing in the centre of the middle boat) gathers his team at Green River, Wyoming, in 1871.*

SHEER SPLENDOUR *The Colorado river is dwarfed by the rock walls of the Grand Canyon.*

The statistics can only begin to indicate the majesty of this vast, silent landscape. The winding slit of the canyon creates a dramatic and ever-changing spectacle of light and shadow, truncating the daylight hours that pass between the cool mists of a lingering dawn to the red and orange fireworks of sunset. As with the Escalante, the valley floor is spattered with greenery wherever the variable flow of the river water permits. Shrubs and gnarled trees help to draw the

eye to a point of focus and give some vague notion of the scale of the dizzying immensity of the rock walls on either side. Animals that thrive in this environment include coyotes, foxes, bobcats and badgers. They also include two different subspecies of tasseleared squirrel, one living on the canyon's North Rim, the other on its South Rim.

CLIMATE TRAPS

Just as large rocks at the back of a beach can give rise to small suntraps, sheltered against the blast of bracing sea breezes, so fiords and deep valleys that run down to inlets by the sea can create their own climatic pockets. Milford Sound is the best-known part of the Fiordland National Park covering 4821 sq miles (12 486 km²) of the south-western part of the South Island of New Zealand. This is a remote wilderness of mountains and lakes, and sheltered inlets carved out by glaciers hundreds of thousands of years ago. The land is warmed by humid westerly winds, and drenched by more than 236 in (6000 mm) of rain every year (one of the highest rainfalls in the world). The scene

MIRROR STILL *Mitre Peak rises over the green-clad hills surrounding Milford Sound (top). Sutherland Falls trickle forth from Lake Quill (above).*

forms a marked contrast with the coastal plains that fringe most of the rest of the South Island.

At Milford Sound the sea runs 12 miles (19 km) inland from its mouth where Mitre Peak rises sheer from the ocean to altitudes of 5550 ft (1691 m). It is now a beauty spot of world renown, visited by thousands of tourists every year many of whom follow a 34 mile (55 km) trek to its head. This passes through a landscape of tussock grass, alpine herbs and mountain beech, mixed with flowering shrubs normally associated with more temperate latitudes, such as broom, senecio and fuchsia. Lower slopes are coated with temperate rain forest, shaggy with beard-like lichen and overhanging the rivers swollen with rain. Sutherland Falls at the head of Arthur River, draining from the lip of Lake Quill, drops 1904 ft (580 m) – making it the tenth highest waterfall in the world.

The Fiordland National Park provides a refuge for the now rare flightless birds of New Zealand, such as the takahe, kiwi and kakapo. It is also home to the world's only mountain parrot, the kea, a model of adaptability which has survived the onslaught of introduced species – and concerted extermination campaigns by farmers because of its habit of pecking sheep to feed off their fat. This cunning bird has learned to feed off anything, and will scavenge from trash heaps, stealing whatever might be mistaken for food – even ski hats and gloves left unattended.

Glacial action also created the wooded shores and inlets of the Cordillera Sarmiento de Gambo, a remote peninsula of southern Chile. Condors wheel over the valleys among the snow-capped peaks. These rise to over 7000 ft (2133 m), spilling glaciers down their slopes and into valleys which thread a path to the sea. While these glaciers calve

CHEEKY CHARLIE *The kea's brazen stealing arouses both fury and affection among humans.*

miniature icebergs into the misty fiords, the shores are packed with dense and rich green rain forest, with thick fern carpets, and beech and cypress trees draped with shaggy mosses.

Thousands of tons of ice in a glacier naturally affect the temperature of the neighbouring land. But where sun traps

THE LOST BIRD

Even before European settlers arrived in New Zealand, its native flightless birds had come under pressure from Maori hunters and their domestic animals. The takahe, a flightless rail, was already rare when first reported by European naturalists – by the 1890s it was believed to be extinct. In 1948, the ornithologist G.B. Orbell made a thrilling discovery. In a valley of the Murchison Mountains, in Fiordland National Park, he found a surviving colony. The next year ornithologists found a population of 200 pairs. Still under the threat of extinction, they have been carefully protected ever since.

create small pockets of warmth, these can support a surprising range of wildlife. High in the Andes, on the border between Argentina and Chile, is the Los Glaciares National Park, where the Moreno Glacier – one of nine in the park – slides into Lake

Argentino. The weather here can be bitter, yet the forests and valleys within the park are home to parakeets and hummingbirds, as well as the pudu – just 14 in (36 cm) high and the smallest deer in the world.

VALLEYS IN MINIATURE

Microclimates – pockets of climate at odds with the climate surrounding them – can be truly minute. Even an unpromising fold in a rock wall may provide enough soil, warmth, moisture and shelter for a wind-blown seed to prosper and take root, attracting a microcosm of insects and other creatures.

The Burren in County Clare on Ireland's west coast presents a forbidding landscape of grey limestone pavements, streaked with ankle-turning fissures. It could be a moonscape – so unaccommodating that Edmund Ludlow, a general in Cromwell's devastating military campaign in Ireland in 1649-50, condemned it as 'yielding neither water enough to drown a man, nor a tree to hang him, nor soil enough to bury him'. Yet plants have found enough moisture and shelter to grow in the fissures, and over the centuries have gradually built up shallow layers of soil in the base of them.

The result is extraordinary. Of the 1400 plant species known in Ireland, 1100 are found on the Burren – and indeed this

GREAT AND SMALL *The Moreno Glacier in southern Argentina grinds through Los Glaciares National Park, home also to the diminutive pudu (above).*

unlikely setting has one the richest ranges of flora anywhere in Europe. Among them are foxgloves, small orchids, pinks and thrifts, which are present elsewhere along this coast.

The climate varies from that of exposed rock faces, lashed by Atlantic winds, to little nooks of warmth oriented to make the most of any sunlight. These may be within a few yards of each other, with the result that alpines such as mountain avens and gentian can be found growing close to Mediterranean plants such as bloody cranesbill and maidenhair ferns.

HERE TODAY, GONE TOMORROW

All environments are subject to change. Microclimates, which often depend on finely balanced variations of the surrounding climate, may come and go over time, and are sometimes the cause of their own annihilation – if, for example, the expansion of roots contributes to the erosion of a river bank. But such changes usually evolve slowly – geological time is so long that by human standards it often passes for permanence.

There are river valleys, however, that regularly undergo dramatic transformation.

BOLD AND DELICATE *Tiny alpine plants such as mountain avens (below) lie cradled in fissures in the limestone pavement of the Burren (left).*

VALLEY OF THE OLD ONES

Few places speak so eloquently of humankind's delicate relationship with landscape as the Canyon de Chelly (pronounced 'shey') in Arizona. Today this is Navajo territory, in a reservation that spans the arid lands on the borders between Arizona, Utah and New Mexico. But the Navajo are comparative newcomers. Around

AD 300, the fertile river banks were worked by people in transition from hunting-gathering to settled village life and farming. They are known simply as the Anasazi, the 'Ancient Ones'. Later they built grand and intricate towns with multistorey houses and ceremonial chambers called *kivas*, at Pueblo Bonito and at cliff settlements

at Mesa Verde. Then, around 1200, they disappeared, perhaps driven away by drought.

The Navajo came to the area in around 1500, perhaps from western Canada. In the 18th century some of them resettled the Canyon de Chelly, farming sheep and growing maize in the protection of the mighty 1000 ft

(300 m) canyon walls – until the defeat of the Navajos by the US army under Colonel Kit Carson in 1864. The Canyon de Chelly is now preserved as a national monument.

CLIFF DWELLERS *For nearly 2000 years people made their homes in the Canyon de Chelly.*

THIRST QUENCHER *Trees lining a creek in north-west Australia make the most of the seasonal rains before the riverbed dries.*

This takes place seasonally in many rivers, when the upper reaches become swollen with meltwater or heavy rains. The results are usually predictable – so predictable in the case of the River Nile in ancient Egypt, and before the completion of the Aswan High Dam, that a civilisation could evolve on the strength of the crops grown in the fertile silt brought by the annual flood.

In some places, the effects are unpredictable. In the desert, goes an old axiom, never camp in a wadi – the Arabic term for a dried-up riverbed in North Africa and the Middle East. Even if the weather looks settled and dry, the wadi could suddenly, without warning, fill with a torrent of water, making the surrounding desert flourish briefly with green vegetation. The cause is heavy rains, falling on mountains which may be many miles away. As the water rushes down the mountain slopes it skates across the surface of the parched, unstable soil, following an erratic course along a path of least resistance.

LUSH GREENERY *Plant and animal life flourish around a billabong in Queensland.*

A similar phenomenon happens in the Australian desert, where seasonally dry watercourses are known as creeks. Fed mainly by the mountains of the Great Dividing Range, the flow and path of these seasonal rivers may be as erratic as that of the wadis, spilling over low banks to convert the landscape into swathes of red mud the size of European countries. Some, however, are well enough established to earn a name and a place on the map, and here and there water remains throughout the year in sidestreams which go by the Aboriginal term 'billabong'. In a year of heavy rains, the watercourses will feed into the salt lakes of central Australia, such as Lake Eyre, and then evaporate – the effect of this is to concentrate the minerals, including salt, in the remaining water.

Wherever the supply of water is sufficient, and sufficiently regular, surprising clusters of life may congregate in and around the creeks. The key elements are usually gum trees – coolabahs and red gums, the most common of the Australian eucalyptus trees. With root systems extensive enough to exploit underground moisture, the red gums can survive long periods of aridity – yet they will only reproduce in the swamp-like conditions that engulf it after flooding.

Stands of red gums will attract a variety of animals that can tolerate these specialist conditions – such as dragonflies, large orb-web spiders, the emperor gum moth which produces caterpillars 6 in (15 cm) long, and even sugar gliders (marsupials that can glide from tree to tree using flaps of skin along their flanks) and ringtail possums.

THE WORLD BELOW

Tunnels, caves and cathedral-like halls sparkling with crystals – some of the Earth's most fantastic landscapes lie beneath its surface. Here are worlds where strange creatures have evolved, sightless and colourless, finding their way in darkness.

Speleology, the scientific exploration of caves, began in earnest just a century ago. Today, cavers forge ever deeper into the world's cave systems – in places as diverse as Europe, Mexico and the heart of the Borneo jungle. But with so many caves blocked off by rock falls and treacherous underground rivers, only a tiny proportion have been fully explored – and countless numbers remain yet to be discovered.

Even with state-of-the-art diving gear, it takes nerves of steel to plunge into an underground river when already four or five days' journey from the surface and depending for air and light on the equipment you are carrying with you. There is the constant danger of accidents in the cave's unpredictable terrain, of equipment failing and of becoming disorientated by the darkness and the absence of night and day. Sudden underground floods are another danger, turning the caves into storm drains.

Yet the rewards of such expeditions may be immense. Quite suddenly a narrow passage may open out into a vast hall, apparently supported on soaring, creamy-white pillars of tapering stalactites and stalagmites. Its walls may be draped with astonishing folds of rock looking more like flowing liquid than rock, the whole scene perhaps reflected in the mirror-still waters of an underground lake.

The living world can add to the catalogue of spectacular surprises. In many New Zealand caves – most famously the Waitomo Cave, 100 miles (160 km) south of Auckland – the dark ceilings are spangled like a starry night with pinpricks of light emitted by millions of tiny glow-worms: the larvae of a cave-dwelling fly, *Arachnocampa luminosa*. But like much else in the dark world of cave life, the reality of this remarkable effect is less romantic. The larvae, housed in sticky tubes of mucus, emit a luminescent glow that attracts midges and other insects into a fatal trap. Their victims fly into the scores of beaded threads of mucus hanging down from the ceiling and become stuck. The larvae then wind them in on the threads and feed off them.

THE WONDERS OF KARST

Almost all the world's major cave systems are found in limestone regions – craggy areas of countryside, often also associated with gorges and semi-barren limestone pavements. Such deeply eroded limestone areas have been given the name karst, after the German for the Kras plateau in Slovenia, part of the Dinaric Alps which run down the coast through Croatia, Bosnia and Albania. This area contains Europe's largest expanse of karst landscape, and includes the

STAR ATTRACTIONS *Visitors view the wonders of Slovenia's Postojna caves (right). At New Zealand's Waitomo Cave (left) the glow emitted by fly larvae draws tourists as well as prey.*

spectacular caves of Postojna, in Slovenia, with 11 miles (18 km) of stalactite-hung caves. One of these is the famous Concert Hall, which has proved large enough for a full orchestra to perform within it.

Perhaps the most remarkable example of this kind of eroded limestone lies in southern China in the Guilin Hills, famous

---

GRISLY REMAINS

The most famous of the natural wells or *cenotes* in the Yucatán Peninsula is the Cenote Sagrada (sacred *cenote*) of Chichén Itzá. Numerous legends surround it, including one that girls were sacrificed there to please Chac Mool, the rain god. There was no evidence to back this up until the US archaeologist Edward H. Thompson began excavations in 1905. Using deep-sea diving equipment, he recovered dolls, jewellery and a decorated gold dish, all of which had presumably been thrown into the well to propitiate the god. He also found numerous skeletons – the skeletons of women.

---

for their towering pinnacles of karst which are spectacularly reflected in the limpid waterways that curve around the flat lands and paddy fields at their feet. The erosion is not simply external: this extraordinary landscape is also riddled with caves.

Limestone is the compacted remains of billions of corals and shellfish and the skeletons of other sea creatures that accumulated over millions of years at the bottom of the

---

LIMESTONE AND WATER *China's Guilin Hills rise from the surrounding waterways.*

sea. It is light and porous. Rain tends to be absorbed by it, leaving the surface comparatively dry. In the Yucatán region of eastern Mexico, there are no rivers at all. Rain disappears rapidly into the limestone crust, leaving the surface dry and barren. Instead, it collects in underground pools. Where accessible from the surface, these pools provided vital freshwater wells, called *cenotes*, upon which whole communities of farmers

KARST SYSTEM *The surface of arid limestone pavement conceals a labyrinthine world beneath, sculpted by the power of water.*

once depended. The *cenotes* were essential to the survival and prosperity of the Maya, whose civilisation spread across the peninsula after about AD 300. The city of Chichén Itzá, for example, depended on the *cenotes* for its water supply. Indeed, the city's very name may refer to this: *chi* in Maya meant 'mouths', and *chen* meant 'wells'.

Rainwater percolates through limestone until it meets a harder stratum of rock. There it will accumulate and form underground streams, which gradually carve ever-larger channels through the soft limestone in their path. Huge chambers may be excavated in

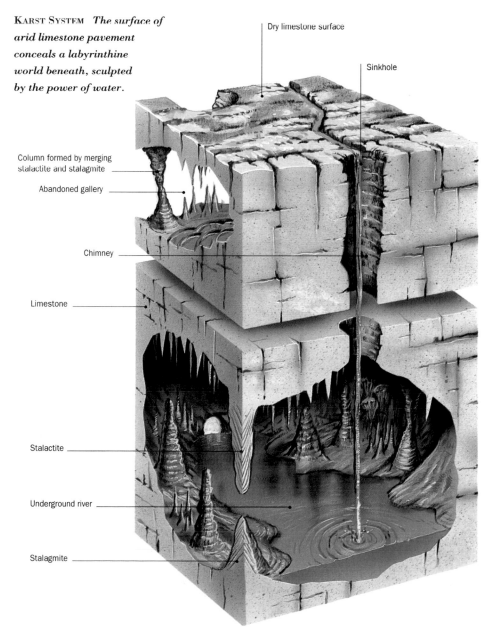

Dry limestone surface

Sinkhole

Column formed by merging stalactite and stalagmite

Abandoned gallery

Chimney

Limestone

Stalactite

Underground river

Stalagmite

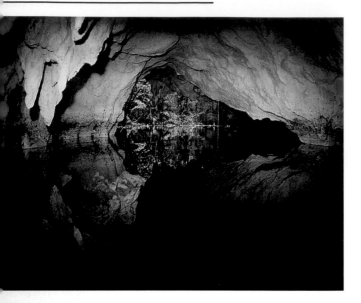

NATURAL WELL *Holes in the limestone crust of the Yucatán Peninsula give access to the water in the* cenotes.

this way, to be filled with lakes. At some point, however, the base of the lake and streams may become eroded, allowing the water to drain away. The result is a dry – or at least damp – cave system.

Meanwhile, water continues to seep through the limestone from above. Mixed with carbon dioxide from the air and soil, it becomes a very mild form of carbonic acid, capable of dissolving the calcite (calcium carbonate) in the rock. As the water drips through the ceiling of a cave, the carbon dioxide evaporates, leaving behind tiny deposits of calcite. Gradually over many, many years, these residues build up to form stalactites – or stalagmites where calcite-laden water drops fall to the floor before evaporating.

Stalactites grow at a rate of about 1 in (2.5 cm) in 500 years – yet some of the largest stalactites are more than 20 ft (6 m) long, representing tens of thousands of years of growth. Clusters dripping down rock walls, with the support of the rock, grow even larger. 'Frozen Niagara' is the name given to a spectacular example of such a group in the world's largest-known cave system, the 'Mammoth Cave' in the state of Kentucky. This has some 294 miles (473 km) of underground passages, caverns and lakes.

Calcite can create other strange wonders, such as smooth, curvaceous globules, unusually regular in shape. New Mexico's Lechuguilla Caves are famous for their huge clusters of stalagmite pillars rising 50 ft (15 m) high, but here the calcite also forms beautiful rounded encrustations in moving water. Like the pearl inside an oyster, these build up in accumulated layers around fragments of rock or bat bones. They are also continuously shaped and smoothed by the water running over them. Even more fascinating are Lechuguilla's gypsum 'flowers' – crystals of calcium sulphite that form needles and flakes of an incredible beauty

PALACES FOR THE SNOW QUEEN

Stalactites and stalagmites have often been compared to icicles, frozen in time. But real ice caves do exist, forming sparkling, crystal chambers filled with glancing light. Many of these are temporary, created by meltwater running through a glacier, or by the hot gas or steam released by a volcanic fumarole into a blanket of snow and ice. Usually these ice caves are destined to collapse when the ceiling becomes too thin to support itself.

Water seeping into limestone cave systems may also become frozen in places where subzero temperatures persist well after the winter has ended on the surface. In the Eisriesenwelt of central Austria huge, frozen cascades of icicles, formed by incoming spring meltwater, fill many of its 25 miles (40 km) of halls and galleries.

But perhaps the most ravishing spectacle among ice caves occurs when warm air from the outside meets the walls of a cavern which are at freezing temperatures after the winter. The warm air turns to ice on contact with the walls, then builds up layers of ice crystals – like enlarged snowflakes, but so delicate that the presence of human warmth can cause their immediate collapse.

HOT AND COLD *An ice tunnel bores through New Zealand's Tasman Glacier. Volcanic steam has created strange shapes on Mount Erebus in Antarctica (below).*

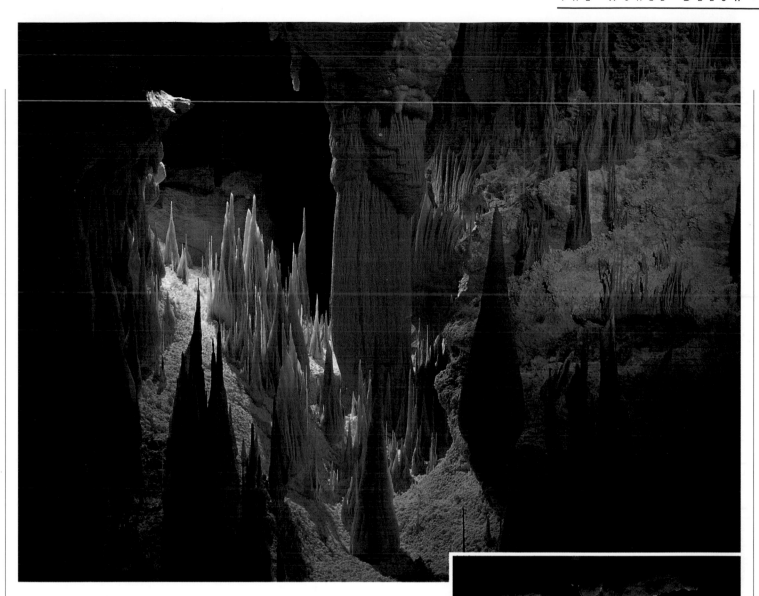

and delicacy, like three-dimensional versions of the ice flowers that appear on window-panes in winter.

WHERE A CAVE IS HOME

A remarkable range of animals live in caves – indeed, every phylum, or major group, of animal life is represented in caves in one form or another. Some of these are highly specialised to cave life, yet none has evolved entirely within the cave environment. They have all come in from the outside – albeit many generations ago.

Many cave-dwelling animals use caves only temporarily, to find shelter in the cold winter months or seek refuge in summer. Racoons, in common with many other mammals, like to give birth to their young in the darkness that a cave can provide. Prehistoric animals, including humans and their immediate forebears, were similarly attracted to caves. The caves' generally stable climatic conditions mean that remarkable remains have been found in them. Among the most celebrated animal finds are the bones and skin of a ground sloth in a cold and dry cave in Patagonia, Argentina. These huge animals grew to be about 23 ft (7 m) tall, and died out only some 5000 years ago. An unusual heritage has survived in the dry conditions of the Bechan Cave in Utah: a layer of dung, 16 in (40 cm) deep, left behind by Columbian mammoths seeking refuge there 13 500 to 11 700 years ago. Analysis of this deposit has proved a valuable resource to scientists studying not just the diet of *continued on page 36*

PERFECT PINNACLES *Yellow-tinted stalagmites (top) and clusters of crystallised gypsum (above) are among the wonders of the Lechuguilla Caves.*

CAVE LIFE

Three features of cave life set it apart from any other habitat. Except for the area close to the entrance, caves are completely dark all of the time – therefore there is no sense of night and day. They are cold and usually damp, but the temperature tends to remain constant. There is virtually no food inside a cave, except what is brought in by animals – or the animals themselves.

Almost all the animals and plants in caves live within the area of half-light close to the cave mouth. Large mammals – such as bears and mountain lions – may find shelter here in winter, as humans did in prehistoric times. Bats hang from the ceiling, sometimes in thousands. Insects, such as springtails, fungus gnats, cockroaches and grylloblattids, feed off the accumulation of bat dung, along with insect larvae and worms. These attract other temporary visitors to the cave mouth, such as frogs, lizards, snakes and mice. Spiders and centipedes also make their homes in this half-lit world.

The damp recesses of caves are home only to the real specialists. Where there is no light, eyesight and pigmentation are useless. Over the millennia specialist creatures have evolved, such as tiny blind fish so transparent that their internal organs can be seen through their skin; blind salamanders and colourless crabs; and species of crickets and beetles which have huge antennae to sense the world around them. They feed off the roots of trees and plants that penetrate the cave from above. Other food comes from fungi and bacteria, bat dung and fragments of organic matter from other animals in the cave. They also eat each other.

DEGREES OF DARKNESS *Blind, pigmentless creatures live in the darkest recesses of caves. Others, such as bats, stay closer to the half-light of the mouth.*

mammoths, but the ecology of the region in ancient times.

Bears, porcupines, rats, mice, nesting birds, snakes, lizards and geckos are all drawn to the shelter of caves. The damp mouth of the Tamana Caves, set among the high rain forest in central Trinidad, attracts freshwater land crabs, an aggressive opossum called a manicou, huge centipedes and the bright green highwoods coral snake. These are all

ECHOLOCATION *Insect-eating bats emit ultrasonic pulses and interpret the 'echoes'.*

troglophiles – cave lovers, as opposed to troglobites, the fully adapted cave-dwellers.

A few bird species have likewise adapted to cave life. The oilbird or guáchero, related

to the nightjar, is found in large numbers in Caripe Cave in Venezuela, where it nests among the stalactites. Swiftlets make their homes in the Mulu Caves of Sarawak, on the island of Borneo. This cave system, lying in the midst of tropical forest, also boasts the world's largest underground cavern, which rises to a height of 230ft (70m).

The archetypal troglophile is the bat. Bats are brilliantly adapted to cave life. Their powers of echolocation allow them to fly in the darkness, and find roosts on the cave ceiling, where they pass the daylight hours. In the case of insect-eating bats this echolocating mechanism is so finely tuned that by emitting 200 signals a second through the nose they are able to detect the position and flight paths of tiny insects in the night sky. The power of this navigational tool becomes even more apparent in a place like Bracken Cave in San Antonio, Texas, home

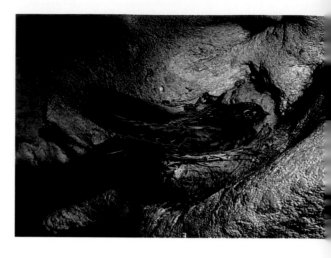

CAVE SAFETY *The cave swiflet of South-east Asia builds a nest of saliva and regurgitated food.*

to 20 million free-tailed bats, the largest single colony in the world. At dusk during the summer months, the entire colony empties through the mouth of the cave and for hours the sky is blanketed by clouds of darting bats. At the end of the night, after clearing the sky of literally tons of insect life, they likewise have to funnel back in through the mouth of the cave, where they pack the ceilings, coating it with a bizarre, fidgeting layer of felt and leather. The navigational abilities of these bats is further put to the test at mating time. These Texas colonies consist entirely of females and pups; the males have their own separate colony in Mexico, 930 miles (1500km) to the south.

Bats play a pivotal role in the ecology of the interior of many caves. Fruit-eating bats forage in the open air at night and then drop seeds on the cave floor on their return. From these seeds miniature forests of spindly and sickly plants grow up. But far more important is the bat dung, which accumulates in deep and pungent layers beneath any sizable colony. A number of creatures feed off this guano, such as insect larvae, worms, ticks and beetles, and these in their turn provide food for other cave-dwellers – the true troglobites, such as the

TUBES OF LAVA

A precise account of events that took place thousands of years ago can be read from the side of a lava tube. These are caves like no others, usually sweeping downhill in a straight or gently curving path, sometimes for several miles – like some huge, roughly hewn drainage pipe.

Lava tubes are formed on the flanks of volcanoes. Where a lava flow forms a regular path, like a river, the outer crust may cool and harden into an arched ceiling, while the lava continues to flow beneath it. If the volcanic activity ceases abruptly, the last emission of molten lava will pass through tube like an underground train, leaving an empty tunnel behind it.

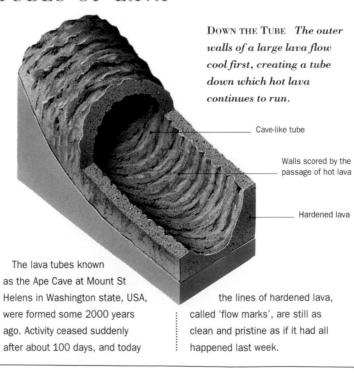

DOWN THE TUBE *The outer walls of a large lava flow cool first, creating a tube down which hot lava continues to run.*

Cave-like tube

Walls scored by the passage of hot lava

Hardened lava

The lava tubes known as the Ape Cave at Mount St Helens in Washington state, USA, were formed some 2000 years ago. Activity ceased suddenly after about 100 days, and today

the lines of hardened lava, called 'flow marks', are still as clean and pristine as if it had all happened last week.

blind salamanders and long-legged eyeless harvestmen, which never see the light of day, and could not survive it if they did.

WHEN CAVES COLLAPSE

The ceiling of a limestone cave may become weakened by drought on the one hand or erosion on the other to such an extent that it can no longer support itself. The result is collapse, which produces a large hole in the ground called a sinkhole. This has been known to occur with dramatic consequences: one sinkhole in central Florida suddenly opened up and swallowed up a house, five cars and part of a swimming-pool complex.

The deep pit of a sinkhole may form its own microclimate. The dry sinkholes of Manitoba in Canada provide the setting for an extraordinary phenomenon. The network of tunnels and caverns connected to them provide refuge for thousands of red-sided garter snakes, which retreat into them to evade the bitterly cold Canadian winter. In spring they emerge from their hibernation,

ART BENEATH THE GROUND

Caves provided refuge for early human beings, and by around 30 000 years ago, they were regularly decorating the walls of these shelters with paintings and relief carvings. The main subjects were animals, such as deer, cattle and mammoths – and many show a remarkable artistic gift for capturing the characteristic postures and physical details of the species depicted.

No one knows for sure what role these works of art played in the lives of their creators, but the drive to produce them was clearly intense. To paint the images high on the walls of the Lascaux cave in France 15 000 years ago, the artists evidently had to construct platforms on scaffolding.

The notion that cave paintings found in France were the work of people living thousands of years in the past was first taken seriously only about 100 years ago. Since then hundreds of examples have been found and each year more are discovered – in France and Spain in particular, but also in Russia and Australia. The remarkable volume of cave art which has survived since prehistoric times invites speculation about just how much of it has been lost through natural deterioration – and how much remains to be found. New discoveries in the pitch-black, far reaches of caves, hundreds of yards from the surface, only deepen the mystery of their function.

COW IN ART *The auroch, an extinct form of cattle, lives on in Stone Age art at Lascaux.*

THAT SINKING FEELING *In 1986 a sinkhole in Columbus, Ohio, caused a huge segment of a main street to collapse.*

and lie in writhing masses in the sinkholes as they re-energise their torpid bodies in the sunshine. They mate and then disperse into the surrounding countryside, where their main diet is frogs, earthworms and slugs. Then they return to the sinkholes in September to begin hibernation. The young, which are born in August, do not go to the sinkholes in their first winter, but only begin to do so the following year. How they learn this habit remains a mystery.

Some sinkholes are filled with water. The Ewens Ponds are among a group of sinkholes in South Australia that are well-known to divers for their spectacularly clear water and unpredictable water currents. Emerald green reeds and pond weed, studded with yellow buttercups, sway in the flowing water, presenting the illusion of tall summer grasses in a wind-raked meadow – except for glimpses of crayfish, eels and aquatic tortoises swimming among them in search of food.

ISLANDS OF LIFE

In their isolation, islands often provide unique conditions for evolutionary adaptations to be played out. Each island has its own geology – that and the forms of natural life which thrive there give the island its own stamp of individuality.

More than 70 per cent of the Earth's surface is covered by oceans. In the midst of the South Pacific, small scattered islands can seem like strange flukes – occurring only where great undersea mountains happen to break the surface. Below the surface lies a world of coral reefs and dramatic underwater cliffs, where multifarious forms of wildlife follow their own agenda. On dry land, above the reach of the tides, is another world, colonised by a mixture of plants and animals which time and the chance of winds and ocean currents have brought together and now left in isolation to devise their own complex set of interrelationships.

Many of the islands of the Pacific are perched on the tip of ancient marine volcanoes – and in the case of the Hawaiian Islands, three of the volcanoes are still active. Some of the most spectacular of

these islands are atolls created by coral that has grown on the flanks of a volcano. Over thousands of years a dense crust builds up, breaking the surface to produce low, rocky strips of land and beach upon which plant life can begin to take hold. Meanwhile, the tip of the volcanic cone and crater subside and erode away, falling back to create a shallow tidal pool called a lagoon, connected to the sea by channels.

The Polynesian island of Bora-Bora, in the same chain as Tahiti, is an example of an atoll in the making. A low-lying ring of coral islands encircles a lagoon, out of which rises the twin-peaked remnant of an inner crater that expired some 3 million years ago.

FADING INTO THE BLUE *Bora-Bora in Polynesia retains its volcanic peak which is slowly collapsing into the sea.*

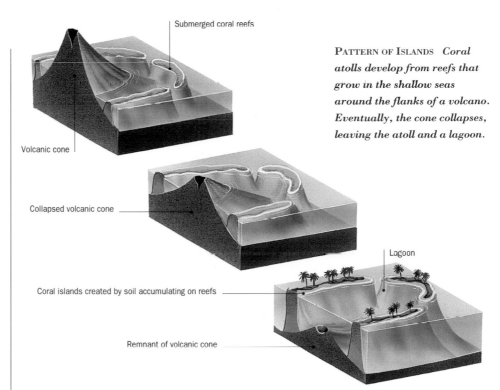

Submerged coral reefs

Volcanic cone

PATTERN OF ISLANDS *Coral atolls develop from reefs that grow in the shallow seas around the flanks of a volcano. Eventually, the cone collapses, leaving the atoll and a lagoon.*

Collapsed volcanic cone

Coral islands created by soil accumulating on reefs

Lagoon

Remnant of volcanic cone

Rising to 2379 ft (725 m) at their highest point, the peaks are often draped with light, fluffy cloud – evidence of the ample rainfall that waters the islands' rich green vegetation. Eventually, however, these peaks will sink away, leaving just the circle of coral islands around the lagoon.

Coral islands are the archetypal 'desert islands'. Bora-Bora is fringed with white sand beaches shaded by palm groves, and dotted with bougainvillea and hibiscus. Dead coral is white and, crushed by the waves, produces dazzling white sand. As the land drops away into the sea, the varying depths are expressed in blue gradations of startling beauty. Similarly spectacular clusters of islands, like gems spread across a jeweller's felt, are formed by the 'heads' of coral reefs in shallow tropical waters – as at Glover's Reef 30 miles (48 km) off the Belize coast in the Caribbean, and in parts of the Maldives in the Indian Ocean.

LAST REFUGE *With no ground predators to fear, flightless rails have been able to survive on Aldabra in the Seychelles.*

Aldabra, in the western Indian Ocean, is the world's largest atoll. It is one of the more remote islands of the Seychelles group, 600 miles (965 km) from the main island of Mahé, and 250 miles (400 km) from both mainland Africa and Madagascar. Located far outside the shipping lanes, and with poor anchorage and little fresh water, it has remained comparatively unscathed. Indeed, a threat by the British to build an air base on the island during the 1960s caused an international outrage because of the damage it would cause to this unique place. The plan was abandoned, and the island is now protected as a World Heritage Site.

LOITERING WITH INTENT
A robber crab of Aldabra uses its powerful limbs to climb a palm for young coconuts.

Aldabra presents an almost complete necklace of jagged coral and eroded limestone. Coconut palms and mangroves grow at the edge of the shallow lagoon, with the tide surging in and out twice a day. These low, dense clumps of greenery offer refuge to powerful robber crabs that are capable of breaking open coconuts with their immense pincers. They owe their name to their habit of raiding the nests of hawksbill turtles, which come ashore from the sea to lay their eggs. The mangroves are also a favoured nesting site for thousands of frigate and booby birds. The male frigates exhibit one of nature's more extraordinary mating rituals. Sitting on their chosen perch, they puff out their huge red throat pouches to attract females. Aldabra also has tiny colonies of two of the world's rarest birds: the Aldabran bush warbler, and flightless Aldabran rail.

Migrating birds are key agents of the colonisation of islands. They bring with them seeds and insects. More insects, seeds, and even spiders, will arrive on the wind. Brazilian moths have reached the island of Tristan de Cunha, 2000 miles (3220 km) away from Brazil in the South Atlantic. Insects, spiders and larger animals, such as reptiles and small mammals, may hitch a ride on lumps of driftwood, or on rafts of floating vegetation, while fertile coconuts and screwpine seeds float like jetsam on the sea and readily germinate when cast up on a beach. Some land animals will swim considerable distances to islands. Aldabra's most celebrated residents are its giant tortoises, which, although essentially creatures of the land, have been known to survive long journeys floating in the sea, and this may explain how they come to be here.

In the absence of any serious challenge from predators, the tortoises have thrived on Aldabra, and they now number 160 000. Over generations they have evolved a comparatively skimpy shell which, at the cost of protection they do not need, allows them greater freedom of movement to feed. Slow and impassive, these giant tortoises can be surprisingly noisy, filling the air with loud, mournful groans during the mating season.

ISLAND LIFE

The Galápagos Islands are the only other place in the world where giant tortoises live in the wild. Situated 600 miles (965 km) west of Ecuador, this collection of five large and eleven small volcanic islands includes strangely tortured landscapes of black rock, as well as the bare red earth of cactus-strewn semidesert, areas of rough grassland, patches of dense scrub, and thickets of giant prickly pear cacti and sunflower 'trees' growing 40 ft (12 m) tall. Although the islands straddle the Equator, the Humboldt Current bringing cold water from the Southern Ocean ensures that they receive low levels of rainfall for this latitude.

The tortoises live on several islands, slumbering through the heat of the day, often in muddy pools where they find some relief from the flies and ticks that prey on them. The males can grow to an immense size, up to 4 ft (1.2 m) long and weighing some 600 lb (272 kg). The females do not usually exceed half this size.

The Galápagos Islands were made famous by the 19th-century English naturalist Charles Darwin, who was the first to recognise the significance of their remarkable wildlife. This includes marine iguanas, flightless cormorants and the world's most northerly species of penguin. But what really caught Darwin's eye were the finches. There are 14 species on the islands – each with features that correspond to their diet. The shape of the beak is particularly telling. Some have strong, small beaks for crushing seeds; others have beaks better suited to tearing at fruit. Some have longer, more pointed beaks for picking insects out of

their hiding places. One species, the woodpecker finch, has even developed an ingenious technique for extracting grubs from the trunks of rotting trees by inserting a cactus spine held in its claw. Since the Galápagos Islands rose from the sea in comparatively recent times, just 2-3 million years ago, all the species on them must be migrants, and hence related to animals that live, or have lived, on neighbouring landmasses. But what could explain the subtle differences in species that have evolved here?

Charles Darwin spent five weeks on the Galápagos Islands in 1835, when he was just 26 years old and serving as the resident naturalist on the round-the-world voyage of a

GALÁPAGOS DEFENCES *Spines on prickly pears (above) fend off hungry tortoises. Walls of black lava (below) offer shelter to nesting flightless cormorants.*

ON THE BEACH *Sally Lightfoot crabs mingle with marine iguanas on the Galápagos Islands (above). The shell of a giant tortoise provides a mobile home for plant life (left).*

naval survey ship, HMS *Beagle*. It took him more than 20 years to assimilate the information he collected on this voyage and to formulate his ground-breaking theory published in 1859: *On the Origin of Species by Means of Natural Selection*. Essentially, he had seen among the Galápagos finches that, over generations, only the most successful animals reproduce. These are the animals that have the features best suited to their environment. Thus the process of evolution works its way out. By this process of natural selection through reproduction, animal species undergo gradual physical changes to adapt to their environment. Those that fail to do so quickly enough to compete will be under threat.

Darwin's theory of evolution was the start of a completely new way of looking at life on Earth. This itself has evolved into the modern approach to ecology, in which life on Earth is seen as a complex web of interdependencies. The different features of animal and plant species are seen in the context of their environment, and explained by the advantages they offer in fulfilling the various requirements of their particular niche in the web of interdependencies.

Small islands, therefore, played a critical role in demonstrating the evolution of modern species. The Galápagos tortoises also provide a good example of the process. Those on the more arid island of Española, for instance, have evolved longer necks so that they can reach the higher branches of the sparse vegetation on that island. Those with shorter necks presumably died. The tortoises, furthermore, belong to a broader community. Lava lizards and vermilion flycatchers eat insects that are attracted to the tortoises, and the tortoises patiently allow finches to pick ticks from their sensitive skin. Mirroring an ancient Hindu legend that the earth is carried on the back of a giant turtle, some of the older Galápagos tortoises even have patches of lichen growing on their shells, which are in turn homes to communities of microscopic organisms.

Larger islands are essentially expanded versions of smaller islands, but their wider, more complex webs of life offer a broader range of conditions in which

species can adapt. In certain cases, isolation has produced wildlife found nowhere else on Earth. Madagascar, cut off from the African mainland for 150 million years, is famous for its unique species, including the tenrec, the fossa, and numerous chameleons and lemurs—including the tiny mouse lemur, at 4 in (10 cm) the world's smallest primate.

New Zealand has its flightless birds, which, without the threat of predators during the centuries before the first humans

HERE ALONE *Madagascar's unique animals include the tenrec (above left), a hedgehog-like relative of moles, and the tiny mouse lemur (above right), no bigger than a human fist.*

ISLAND DWARFS AND MONSTERS

Limited food sources have led to extreme forms of life on some islands. In the Galápagos Islands and on Aldabra in the Seychelles there are giant tortoises. The Indonesian island of Komodo is home to the world's largest lizard, the Komodo dragon. Huge coconut crabs, with leg spans of 2 ft (61 cm) across, inhabit many of the coral atolls of the South Pacific. By contrast, dwarf key deer live on islands off Florida; dwarf hippopotamuses lived on the island of Cyprus in ancient times; and recently the remains of dwarf mammoths have been found on Wrangel Island, in the far north-east of Siberia.

Unlike mainland terrestrial species, island dwellers cannot migrate when food runs low. Where resources are limited, animals that require less food have an advantage; this favours the evolution of smaller species with less bulk to support. If, on the other hand, a species faces no real competition for the food, and no great threat from predators, a larger size will not be a disadvantage – and it will be the larger animals that dominate in mating.

MINIATURES AND GIANTS *Key deer on Florida islands are about half the size of their mainland cousins. Komodo, Indonesia, is home to the 10 ft (3 m) long Komodo dragon, a descendant of the dinosaurs.*

LIVING DINOSAUR *The tuatara survives on a handful of islands off New Zealand.*

arrived around 1300, lost the need to fly. Still more extraordinary is the survival of the tuatara, a horny, lizard-like reptile which is the only living member of its order, the Rhynchocephalia, which flourished 200 million years ago, at the time of the dinosaurs.

This was about the time that Australia became a separate island. It has a spectacularly unusual range of wildlife, including 120 species of marsupials as diverse as the koala, the kangaroos, the sugar glider and the tiny honey possum. It also has the flightless emu and cassowary as well as the world's only monotremes, the egg-laying echidna and duckbill platypus.

HUMAN RAVAGES

No natural environment is ever static. Generally the pace of change is slow; when it quickens, all the environment's different species find themselves under pressure. With their limited range of resources and the specialist habits of their wildlife, small-island ecologies are particularly vulnerable. Major catastrophes that would be local disasters in larger environments – such as tidal waves, volcanic eruption and epidemics – may cause irreversible changes, and rob an island of the means to recover.

The main agent of rapid change, however, is the human race. People have had a dramatic impact on the delicate balances of nature in countless islands. The most famous example is the dodo of Mauritius. This huge pigeon was easy prey for passing ships full of hungry sailors in need of fresh meat. Not only was it flightless: like many species that have no predators to be afraid of, it was tragically friendly. The last was killed in 1681. Sailors were likewise responsible for the annihilation of colonies of giant tortoises on Mauritius, the Comoros Islands and Madagascar, and they came close to wiping them out on Aldabra. Tortoises provided a living larder. Bundled up by the hundreds, they could survive for many months in a ship's hold without food or drink – a tragic fate for an animal that can live for 150 years. The Galápagos

AS DEAD AS . . .

Mauritius was once a stopping point for European ships en route to South Asia and the Far East. Sailors were amazed by a giant, flightless member of the pigeon family. It stood about 4 ft (1.2 m) tall, had soft, blue-grey feathers, a curly tuft instead of a tail, a thick, hooded beak and a quizzical expression. The Portuguese called it *doudu* – stupid. Certainly, it was too friendly for its own good. Dodos, or relatives, had been found on other islands of the southern Indian Ocean, but after the death of the last one on Mauritius in 1681 the only survivors were on the islands of Réunion and Rodrigues. Here they were called solitaires, because they seemed to live alone in the forest. They lasted until about 1800, and then the dodo was truly dead.

tortoises were similarly exploited, and in the 1930s they were killed to extract their fatty oils.

Human impact can also be less direct, but equally dramatic. Species imported by settlers, such as dogs, pigs and rabbits, can destroy the existing equilibrium of an island. Pigs contributed to the demise of the dodo on Mauritius by eating their eggs. Uninvited guests, such as rats, can wreak even greater havoc. Lord Howe Island, lying about 430 miles (700 km) east of Sydney, is today

UNGAINLY BIRD *The dodo was recorded by artists such as Roelandt Savery, who painted this one in 1625.*

SAFETY ON A CRAG *The cliffs of Balls Pyramid (below) protect the nesting sites of birds such as the red-tailed tropic bird (left). Many species have been wiped out on the more accessible Lord Howe Island beyond.*

famous as a getaway holiday resort, and also as the source of the Kentia palm, one of the most attractive of the indoor palms. The island was discovered in 1788 by a British naval lieutenant called Henry Ball, and named after the First Lord of the Admiralty, Lord Howe. Sailors stopping off on

SAFETY IN NUMBERS *Elephant seals (left) converge to breed on the Falkland Islands. Nesting gannets (above) congregate on islands off Ireland.*

the island hunted a variety of tame birds to extinction. Then in 1834 settlers arrived with cats, pigs, goats and mice. The rat arrived in 1918. Between them these animals exterminated many of the island's unique species, including lizards and stick insects.

Within view of Lord Howe Island is the spectacular Balls Pyramid, the world's highest rock pinnacle. This wedge-shaped remnant of a volcano rises sharply from the sea to nearly 1800 ft (550 m) – one and a half times the height of the Empire State Building – and offers no easy landing point. Unlike Lord Howe Island, it remained effectively untouched by the interference of humans or rats, and its rocky ledges are home to remote colonies of wildlife, including lizards, giant centipedes and thousands of nesting seabirds such as boobies and petrels. Another of its birds is the red-tailed tropic bird, which needs isolation to survive. It has so little fear of predators that on other islands people have been able to steal the decorative tail feathers from living birds. But like many

islands that have preserved their ecological integrity, Balls Pyramid has done so by virtue of its inhospitality – and by definition that also means that it will be able to support only a narrow band of specialist dwellers.

This can be seen in an extreme form on islands almost totally dominated by a single species. Some of the sea stacks off Scotland and western Ireland are regularly covered with tens of thousands of nesting birds, such as guillemots in the Orkney Islands, and gannets on the Skelligs off County Kerry. Elephant seals gather in huge numbers to breed on chosen islands around Antarctica, filling the shoreline with their rotund, bulky forms, and the flaky debris of their moulting skin and fur. One of the most extraordinary congregations of a single species occurs each spring on the tiny volcanic island of Zavodovski, in the South Sandwich group in the far south of the Atlantic. Some 14 million chinstrap penguins come here to breed, covering the steep slopes of volcanic ash with black and white swarms. The essential difference between these islands of mass-congregation and others is that the dominant animals do not depend on the island itself for their food – but on the rich pickings to be found in the seas that surround them.

STRANGE WORLDS ON OUR DOORSTEP

The strange worlds created by the microclimates and intimate ecosystems of remote valleys and isolated caves and islands all demonstrate evolution at work. But we do not have to go to far-off places to see such wonders. They are all around us.

A magnifying glass helps to reveal the complexity and beauty of the world on our doorsteps: a spider's web beaded with morning dew; the busy, nervous work of a hoverfly feeding on nectar; the ancient form of a woodlouse's segmented carapace; the glistening contours of snails and their ultrasensitive antennae; the inventive, abstract forms of seeds, ranging from compact spirals to bristling orbs.

Even the most mundane web of life may be extraordinary. A tree grows at the edge of a city garden. It buds in spring, grows its leaves and flowers, produces berries or fruits in late summer, sheds its leaves in autumn. It is a busy year – but this is not even half the story. For a tree is not just a tree, but the focus and starting point for a whole world of activity. Moth and beetle larvae feed on the roots; bark beetles tunnel beneath the bark to lay eggs. Aphids feed off the sap; caterpillars and leaf miners feed off the leaves. Ants

HUNTER AND HUNTED *A ground beetle on some decaying wood sinks its jaws into a grub.*

SOFT TOUCH, HARD SHELL
*A common garden snail (left)
and a woodlouse (above) feel
their way around the world
using their antennae. A dewy
spider's web (below) creates
a lethal mesh of beauty.*

climb the branches to herd the aphids, feasting on their sweet, gluey, honeydew secretion. Ladybird larvae, adult ladybirds and lacewings feed off the aphids. Birds come from far and wide to feed off the insects and the berries. And leaving the tree,

FANTASTIC MICROSCOPIC WORLDS

Strange and fantastic worlds of unearthly beauty come to light under the lens of a powerful microscope. Bacteria, microscopic algae, cell structures and the tiniest details of nature reveal shapes, forms and colours quite unlike anything in the normally visible world. Pollen grains are a case in point. No larger than specks of dust, around just 100 millionths of a millimetre across, they have a spectacular range of shapes and forms – resembling prickly fruits, rugby balls, leather purses, brains, coral, baker's buns, or with shapes that resemble nothing else on Earth.

a lacewing may perhaps be caught in flight by a swallow – a swallow that spends part of its year on the other side of the world.

Microclimates, too, abound, even in the complex ecological environments in which most modern people live. Because of the

COLOUR OF FEAR *Predators that ignore the warning colours of an emperor moth caterpillar (far left) or a ladybird (left) are in for a bitter surprise. The harmless hoverfly (above) depends on a predator's fear of wasps.*

the dead leaf, returning the nutrients to the soil in a form that can be absorbed by living plants – which in turn will provide food and habitats for aphids, ants, bees, snails, mice, birds and all the many other garden visitors.

DARWIN IN THE CITY

The world on our doorsteps also reveals some remarkable evolutionary adaptations. Darwin recognised that animals and plants have to adapt to survive. They have to alter their habits and even their physical make-up to match changing environmental conditions. Remote islands are the best places to see how this works, but cities – in principle, the most unsympathetic environment for animal life – also offer some dramatic demonstrations of the processes in action.

A classic example of natural selection is that of certain city-dwelling moths, such as the engrailed moth. In the past their black

nature of human life – the need for food, equable temperatures, sufficient rainfall – the places where people live are, generally, extremely rich habitats. A garden in a temperate part of the world will contain an extraordinary diversity of life. Under a single dead leaf there might be beetles, small spiders, woodlice, centipedes, earwigs, earthworms, wireworms and a variety of insect larvae, as well as fungi and bacteria.

Each feeds off parts of this tiny microcosm, such as decaying vegetation, living plant material or the other life forms occupying the same minute space. They also form part of the ecology of the world beyond. They break down the structure of

URBAN DRIFT *Adaptable and often generously fed, pigeons are a part of life in many cities, such as Paris (above).*

and white spotted coloration allowed them to remain camouflaged against the bark of a tree. With the growth of industrialisation and consequent air pollution, the trunks of the trees became blackened, and the moths' cover was blown. Now the birds that fed on them could spot them more easily against

IN DEFIANCE OF POLLUTION

Garden plants are remarkably resilient to urban pollution. By definition, they are adaptable and tolerant. Also, plant growth, like pollution, is essentially about chemicals, and plants are indifferent to the source of the chemicals. By most plants' standards, city pollution alters the environment very little. Even acid rain has little effect. When simulated acid rain has been sprayed onto plants, some have actually fared better. That said, all plant life is ultimately sensitive to pollution, on a sliding scale. Few plants can tolerate heavy soil contamination.

their background. The birds, however, failed to see those with a darker coloration that did match the background. These were the ones that survived and reproduced, and as a result whole populations of moths soon became darker in colour.

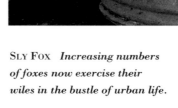

SLY FOX *Increasing numbers of foxes now exercise their wiles in the bustle of urban life.*

Cities, then, just as much as islands or hidden valleys, create their own special worlds. Some larger animals have adapted to the urban environment particularly well. Pigeons are the archetypal city birds, perching on ledges and monuments, and feeding off any edible refuse available.

Sparrows are similarly adaptable, and are found throughout European and North American cities. Brown rats – originally from South-east Asia – have survived more than five centuries of persecution by hiding in drains and sewers. In recent years the red fox has become an increasingly familiar sight in north European cities. Making its home in parks, large gardens and wasteland, it has learned to feed from trash cans and garbage bags. Bats, raccoons and badgers have shown a similar willingness to adapt.

Cities, after all, offer some rich pickings. Predators are comparatively scarce, and the winters are slightly warmer than in the country. Houses offer shelter and food to countless animals besides their ostensible owners. Mice come in from the gardens and railway lines; damp corners attract woodlice. There are spiders, cockroaches, wood-boring beetles, dust mites and bedbugs.

The degree to which animals adapt to environments created by and for humans may be a surprise. Yet in many ways cities and houses reflect the conditions elsewhere. The roofs and eaves of buildings are similar to rock ledges and caves; a skirting board is as good a refuge as a fallen branch. Animals in the city have to learn to accept the disruption of human presence, but by and large either humans are fairly tolerant, or the animals are able to reproduce faster than humans are able to destroy them. In the city, as on the desert island, the same rules of survival and evolution apply.

TEEMING WITH LIFE
2

COMFORTABLE NICHE *A cattle egret takes advantage of the relaxed mood of a hippo.*

WETLANDS AND FORESTS TEEM WITH LIFE. THIS RICH AND DIVERSE EXPRESSION OF THE FORCES OF EVOLUTION DEPENDS ON THE FUNCTIONING OF A GREEN PIGMENT. IN THE PROCESS OF PHOTOSYNTHESIS, GREEN CHLOROPHYLL TRAPS THE ENERGY OF SUNSHINE IN LEAVES TO TURN WATER AND CARBON DIOXIDE INTO SUGARS. THE ORGANIC MOLECULES PRODUCED ARE THE BUILDING BLOCKS OF GROWTH — THE FOUNDATIONS OF PLANT LIFE. PLANT LIFE PROVIDES THE NUTRIENTS TO SUSTAIN MOST OF THE THOUSANDS OF SPECIES THAT MAKE UP THE WORLD'S FOOD WEB. PLANT GROWTH DEPENDS ON SUNSHINE, WARMTH AND MOISTURE — IN WETLANDS AND FORESTS ALL THESE ARE AVAILABLE IN ABUNDANCE.

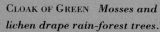

CLOAK OF GREEN *Mosses and lichen drape rain-forest trees.*

WETLAND ABUNDANCE

Rich tangles of plant life thrive in the fertile, sodden world of marshes, swamps and bogs – 'wetlands'. These generous habitats, protected by their inaccessibility, are home to a wide range of animals, uniquely adapted to these conditions.

Marshes, swamps and bogs, thick with reeds and sedges, draped with lichens and moss, are some of the world's richest ecosystems. In warmer climates they provide conditions that are perfect for intense growth – and rich pickings for fish, insects, reptiles, amphibians, birds and mammals. The profusion of growth and the soft, wet terrain serve as effective defences, preserving their remoteness and hindering human access.

Marshes (areas of poorly drained land), swamps (waterlogged land, often partly forested) and bogs (where the sodden ground is spongy with decayed vegetation) are highly unstable, ever-changing environments. Swamps and marshes are often the temporary product of annual rains, which fill rivers, gullies and hollows for a brief period every year and transform the landscape. In salt marshes and coastal mangrove swamps the changes are rung with every tide.

The Sudd is a marshland in the sweltering middle reaches of the White Nile, occupying much of southern Sudan, an area the size of England. Papyrus plants grow in thickets, building up floating islands of decayed vegetation, and creating a mobile maze of channels and dead ends – a navigator's nightmare. The level of the swamp rises and falls dramatically over the year, swollen in December by the rains and melting snows of distant mountains, and evaporating so rapidly through the rest of the year that the Sudd accounts for the loss of a large proportion of the water of the White Nile. The Sudd almost defeated Samuel and Florence Baker on a journey up the Nile in 1861-4. 'Some evil spirit appears to rule in this horrible region of everlasting swamp,' Samuel Baker noted. 'The fabulous Styx must be a sweet rippling brook, compared to this horrible creation.'

Seen another way, this was praise for the natural defences of wetlands. The Sudd is not, of course, so horrible to the crocodiles, hippos, water birds and millions of mosquitoes that make it their home. But like all wetland creatures, they are specialists. The constant presence of water requires tailor-made adaptations. Plants growing in

DESERT ISLANDS *The sandy soil of the Kalahari shows through on the trampled islands of the Okavango Delta in Botswana.*

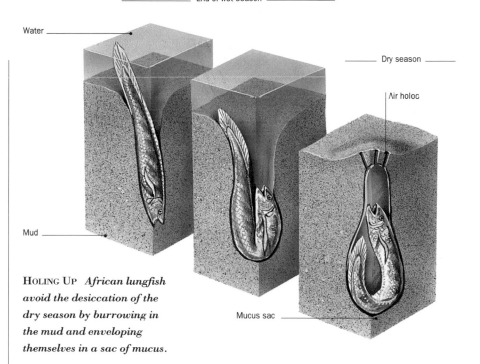

Water

End of wet season

Dry season

Air hole

Mud

Mucus sac

HOLING UP *African lungfish avoid the desiccation of the dry season by burrowing in the mud and enveloping themselves in a sac of mucus.*

waterlogged land have to be water-tolerant hydrophytes, and may need special features to supply air to their roots – like the hollow tubes of papyrus stems. Mosquitoes lay their eggs in or near water, and the larvae and pupae live in water before emerging into the air. Like so many wetland creatures, their lives are fully integrated with the wet and the dry.

Because they are specialists, the animals and plants of the wetlands are vulnerable to a deterioration in their habitat – notably the loss of water. Some have developed extraordinary strategies to survive drought. As the dry season approaches, terrapins and toads of Botswana's Okavango Delta burrow into the mud, while the African lungfish squirms into a muddy subterranean tube, seals itself into an envelope of mucus to reduce water loss, and uses its lung-like swim bladder to breathe oxygen through the top of the hole.

AFRICAN WONDERLAND
One remarkable wetland lies in the middle of southern Africa, where the Okavango River forms the world's largest inland

delta before running into the sands of the Kalahari Desert. Every year heavy rains in the distant mountains of Angola swell the tributaries of the River Cubango, which heads south across the panhandle Caprivi

Strip of Namibia (where it becomes the Okavango) and then enters the flat lands of northern Botswana.

The rains take several months to reach the delta, and so arrive at a time when the surrounding land is beginning to suffer the results of a long dry season. The flood waters flow into the area of permanent swamp in the north, then spread out across the parched land to its south, spilling over the fragile banks of river courses and chasing around low islands on which stands of sycamore, fig trees and fan palms grow. The swamp thus doubles in size for about five months every year, from 4250 sq miles (11 000 km²) to 11 000 sq miles (28 500 km²).

After the rains the Okavango Delta bursts into life. A flourish of papyrus reeds and grasses crowds the banks that line still waterways. Sixty-five species of fish, many of which have survived as eggs and fry in the swampy dry-season pools, grow rapidly in the nutrient-rich flood water – providing food for numerous birds such as African

THE ULTIMATE WETLAND CREATURE

Most aquatic creatures are streamlined to help them to move through water. Streamlining, however, passed the hippopotamus by: hippos are built to wallow. Their eyes, nostrils and ears are positioned on the top of their heads to allow them to rest in the water with their sensory tools just above the surface – though they can stay under water for five minutes. The common hippo can reach a colossal size – up to 15 ft (4.6 m) long, and weighing over 2 tons, three times bigger than its cousin, the pygmy hippo of the West African forests. This scale is feasible when for much of the day it is supported by water. If hippos seem slothful, it is because they have few cares. Adults have no serious predators: they will share the same waters with crocodiles, confident that the crocodiles will leave them alone.

During the day hippos slumber, retiring to the water to avoid the heat of the sun and snacking on aquatic plants such as water cabbage. At dusk they move along well-trodden underwater paths and emerge from the water to graze on pastures, eating up to 330 lb (150 kg) every night to feed their vast bulk. On land

they show that they are not nearly as slothful as they might appear: bull hippos are surprisingly speedy and agile when protecting cows or calves and can overtake a running human.

GROUP THERAPY *Hippos are sociable animals, living together in large family groups.*

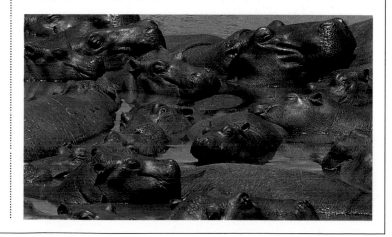

fish eagles, ibises, egrets, herons, pelicans, spoonbills and jaçana birds.

As the land begins to dry out and becomes firmer, one of Africa's greatest concentrations of large mammals begins to move in – giraffes, wildebeest, sitatunga antelopes, lechwes, zebra, warthogs, baboons, Cape clawless otters, lions and hyenas. As the waters recede, the watering holes begin to dry out, creating ever richer concentrations of food for predatory birds and animals. Many of the nesting birds time the rearing of their young to coincide with this glut.

The local San and baYei people have lived among the waters of the delta for hundreds of years, and have an intimate knowledge of its rhythms. However, the delta is now under threat from cattle ranching. Long wire fences protect it from invasion by cattle herders, and protect domestic cattle from the foot and mouth disease carried by wild herds of buffalo and wildebeest. But they also cut across migration paths hampering the natural seasonal movement of wildebeest and other animals.

The Okavango Delta is a fragile world. It lies over a deep layer of sand and is differentiated from the rest of the Kalahari only by its moist blanket of fertile soil, replenished annually by the distant rains. Other nearby lakes have been and gone. Lake Ngami, to the south-east, which David Livingstone saw in 1849, is now a dry salt pan. Consequences such as these demonstrate the vulnerability of wetlands. They are not isolated ecosystems that can be fenced in but vital organs in a wider landscape.

THE HEART OF SOUTH AMERICA

Across the borders of Bolivia, Paraguay and Brazil stretches one of the world's magnificent wetlands, the Pantanal. Each year, between November and March, torrential rains flood the River Paraguay, filling the plains with up to 10ft (3m) of water and turning them into a swamp the size of Great Britain, a playground for one of the world's richest concentrations of freshwater fish – some 350 species in all. Piranhas and caimans prowl about in shallow lagoons, while palm-studded islands provide refuge for parrots, egrets, jabiru storks, cormorants, jaguars,

WATERLOGGED *A great white egret stalks fish and frogs in the marshes of the Pantanal. A marsh deer wades through its soggy meadows in search of the more stable ground.*

deer, monkeys and capybaras – the largest rodents in the world. Then, as the dry season advances, the swamp recedes, losing as much as a quarter of its total area. Water settles in isolated pools which become dense with fish, and a convenient larder for breeding birds and other animals with young mouths to feed.

Over the years cattle ranching has gradually encroached upon the Pantanal. More recently, a canal project has been proposed that would enable ocean-going ships to sail all the way up the Paraná and Paraguay rivers from Buenos Aires to the very heart of South America. The diversion of water to this massive project would have far-reaching consequences on the flow of water which sets the rhythm for this swampland.

BOG LIFE

Will-o'-the-wisp or jack-o'-lantern they called it – fairy-tale names for the mysterious phenomenon of dancing lights that flicker through tar-black nights across marshlands and bogs. They are believed to be caused by the spontaneous combustion of methane and other gases that bubble up through the decaying vegetation. But they play a darker role in the folklore of wetlands. These lights beckon unwary men and women to venture into the mire, where they are pulled by their own weight into the mud and engulfed.

In the distant past, when marshlands and bogs covered far more of the Earth's surface than today, these mysterious landscapes inspired both fear and respect. Religious rites, it appears, were performed on the perimeter of bogs during the Iron Age. Wounds on human bodies found in Denmark, such as Tollund man and Grauballe man – preserved in all their leathery detail by the tannins in the wet soil – suggest that they may have been human sacrifices.

Marshes are landscapes dominated by reeds and grasses; mosses and heathers dominate bogs. There are bogs across much of the northern, temperate parts of the world – from Ireland and Finland to Siberia and Canada. Bogs take about 5000 years to develop on land which is constantly water-logged by rainfall. First of all shrubs, such as alder and willow, grow around the edges of a pool, and then these are overwhelmed by sphagnum moss, heathers and sedges. The lack of oxygen in the stagnant water slows down decay, but over the centuries dead vegetation forms a deep, compact layer of spongy, waterlogged debris, and eventually turns into peat.

Ireland has two sorts of bog: blanket bog found mainly in the coastal regions of the west; and raised bog, which consists of shallow hillocks that have built up over inland hollows left behind by the retreat of glaciers 12 000 years ago. Many of these pockets of wet, awkward terrain have been left more or less untouched for centuries, providing sanctuaries for dragonflies, frogs, otters, larks and snipe, and numerous migrating birds such as Greenland geese. Iridescent oils sparkle on the surface of the still, darkly glinting pools of water, while delicate bog-land plants catch the light of a westering sun – the tufted head of bog cotton, pink pimpernel and bog asphodel, sturdy orchids, and the glistening sundew which supplements the nutrient-starved soil with meals of insects lured to its dribbling nectar.

Peat – or 'turf' as it is called in Ireland – is a kind of juvenile coal, an effective fuel long used as a way of warming the hearths and cooking ranges of Irish cottages. It is still extracted and cut into compact briquettes, dried through the summer in neat pyramids and then stacked outside before the winter. More recently peat has been put to industrial use, to fuel power stations.

THE RIVER OF GRASS

Some of the world's most remarkable wetlands lie across the south-east of the USA. Many of these are swamps, which here are defined as wetlands dominated by trees and large shrubs, such as cypress, tupelo

DARK WATERS *Bog asphodel, orchids and heather crowd round the peat-blackened water of a bog in the Scottish Highlands.*

and magnolia. In the Okefenokee swamps of south-eastern Georgia, a dense canopy of leaves shuts out the light from the dim and dank world below. Islands of decaying vegetation float on the surface of the water, giving rise to the swamp's Indian name, which means 'trembling earth'.

Like the Okavango Delta, these swamps undergo seasonal transformations. The Atchafalaya swamp in the Louisiana Bayou country, for example, changes between the lush greenness that follows the spring floods,

and the autumn, when its deciduous trees open the drying waterways to the sky.

The most famous of the US wetlands is the Florida Everglades. This was once a wetland like no other – a kind of river no more than 3 ft (1 m) deep but 50 miles (80 km) wide which tipped down the gentle tilt of a limestone plateau from Lake Okeechobee to the south coast of the peninsula. It was shallow enough for sawgrass to grow in aquatic meadows, bent to the flow of the water – the 'river of grass' as it was called.

In the wet season from June to October the Everglades fill to become a vast, shallow pond, broken by bands of reeds and low pineland ridges. In the dry season the waters recede. Animals such as white-tailed deer, marsh rabbits and black bears come out of the shelter of tree-decked islands and venture into the damp prairies, scattering clouds of grasshoppers and butterflies. Other areas remain dark swamplands, shaded by cypress trees swathed in a tangle of bromeliads, ferns and hanging moss, and providing moist retreats for snakes, alligators and large, tree-climbing snails. Around the coastal fringe are bands of mangrove swamps, home to American crocodiles and egrets.

The Everglades have been under threat for decades. The Everglades National Park was created in 1947 in the south-western quadrant. However, it does not include the waterways linking it to Lake Okeechobee, and the flow of water through the park is controlled by gates – a system that cannot mirror the natural rhythms on which this ecosystem once depended. Many of its animal species are now endangered.

The Everglades National Park is an inhospitable world for humans – with an oppressively humid climate and plagues of mosquitoes. But it offers a safe habitat for numerous birds, such as roseate spoonbills, egrets, anhingas and red-shouldered hawks. On the dry islands are black bears, marsh rabbits and the rare Florida panther. The estuaries attract a most endearing aquatic mammal, the gentle, rotund, vegetarian manatee, a distant relative of the elephant.

The archetypal Everglades animal is the alligator. The Spanish conquistadores would have encountered it in Florida as they searched for gold and land in the 16th century. They called it *el legarto*, the lizard, from which our word is derived. Besides the American alligator of the south-eastern USA, the only other group of alligators in the world lives in China, on the upper Chang Jiang (Yangtze river). Their exposed upper teeth, when the mouth is closed, distinguish them from crocodiles, which usually show both sets of teeth.

continued on page 62

BAYOU COUNTRY *Thick hanks of Spanish moss hang from the branches of the bald cypress trees in the Atchafalaya swamp of Louisiana.*

WETLANDS UNDER THREAT

Humans have always been at odds with wetlands. They find them an obstacle to travel, or an opportunity for development which, by drainage, could be turned into productive pasture or building land.

Since the 17th century all wetlands have been on the retreat. The Dutch drained their coasts to create the polders for pasture and cereal crops, then brought their expertise to the Fens of eastern England. Gradually the great swamplands of south-eastern USA have been drained and squeezed into ever smaller pockets to produce agricultural land on the rich swampland soil; and latterly marshes have been corralled into picturesque waterfront housing developments. It is estimated that 300 000 acres (121 500 ha) of US wetlands are lost every year, and, significantly, one-third of all the endangered species in the USA are wetland creatures. Peat is being extracted from bogs and exploited as a fuel or garden fertiliser not only in Ireland, but in places as far apart as Russia, Burundi, Jamaica and Indonesia.

Everywhere in the world wetlands are under threat, as these apparently marginal areas of land come under the dual pressure of population expansion and economic exploitation. The defence of wetlands has become a burning ecological issue. Two

THREATENED *Everglades apple snails are declining in numbers thanks to drainage schemes.*

arguments are used in their support: first, they are uniquely rich habitats, providing havens for densely packed and immensely diverse species, many of which are threatened with extinction if their habitat is destroyed. Second, many of these wetlands may in fact be most productive in their wetland state. They form part of integrated, natural water and drainage systems which are often too complex and fragile to bear human tinkering – the ecological balance of the Everglades

RARE GLIMPSE *Big Cypress Swamp, adjoining the Everglades, is one of the last refuges of the Florida panther.*

is being upset as drainage projects cause salt water to flow into previously freshwater areas. Salt marshes also provide spawning grounds for a number of species of shrimp, crab and fish upon which many commercial fishing fleets depend. Humans play with wetlands at their peril.

TIDAL SHIFTS

Twice a day the world of the tidal salt marsh is transformed by the invasion and retraction of the sea. It is the setting for an ever-repeated drama performed by succeeding shifts of players, according to their preferred mix of water, salt, air and mud. Salt marshes are one of the richest interfaces between land and sea. They occupy flat lands, protected from the waves by the shoreline, where silt-laden freshwater streams meander towards the sea. The incoming tide halts the flow of water in the streams, making them deposit their silt. This builds up into banks of mud, where eel grass and kelp take root. As soon as the banks are high enough to be exposed to the air, they are ready for further plant colonisation: glasswort (or marsh samphire) can take root on a mudbank if it is exposed for just three hours. Cordgrass and other spartinas also thrive. A host of sturdy, salt-tolerant plants such as sea pinks, sea asters and common scurvy grass grow in the firmer soil, and create the characteristic spongy turf that cloaks the higher ground around salt marshes. Each layer of this rich ecosystem is occupied by its specialists, from the cockles and mussels in the mud, to the grasshoppers and beetles in the marsh turf.

CAMOUFLAGE *Flounders are almost invisible unless they move. All fish in salt marshes have to tolerate variations in the water's salt content; flounders adjust the salinity within their bodies.*

FILTER SYSTEMS *Mussels, razor shells and other bivalves feed by filtering particles from rich tidal waters. Mussels remain half-submerged in the mud, protected by their tough shells. Razor shells withdraw deep into the mud.*

HOME LOAN *A hermit crab adopts the discarded shells of other sea creatures. As it becomes larger, it will seek a new shell.*

HIGH TIDE *Ducks, swans and geese are drawn to the pools of water that form at high tide, feeding on weed, insects and molluscs. The marsh turf and banks of reeds make good nesting sites. Some fish thrive in the brackish water, such as sticklebacks and roach, while sea fish such as flounders and mullet come in on the tide.*

LOW TIDE *The ebbing tide reveals mud, braided by rivulets of fresh water draining from inland. Curlews, avocets, rails and oystercatchers flock in, digging for shellfish or ragworms, or searching in the grasses and kelp for insects. The drained land offers a firmer foothold for mammals such as otters and racoons. The tide has also flushed the salt-marsh detritus into the sea, providing a wealth of nutrients for marine creatures along the shore.*

FLYING IN *Low tide offers rich pickings for coastal birds, especially the seagull. Herring gulls are a success story of adaptation – happy to follow the plough for worms as well as seeking fish and shellfish.*

SAVOURY OR SWEET *Many species of crab – shore crabs, fiddler crabs and blue crabs – are ideally suited to life on the tidal margins, able to survive in water and out, and in both salt and brackish water.*

Growing to about 10 ft (3 m) long, the Everglades alligators spend much of the day slumbering on the muddy banks of the islands. They live in semisubmerged dens, but in the spring the female builds a nest, 7 ft (2 m) wide, out of mud and leaves, and lays 30-40 eggs in it. The sun's warmth incubates the eggs, which hatch after ten weeks. The female then pulls the nest apart to release the young. If any of her young cannot break open its egg, the female takes it into her mouth and crushes the shell to release the baby alligator – a task that requires great tenderness. Later, young alligators will often ride on their mother's back.

Alligators also live in the Big Cypress swamp to the north-west of the Everglades. This subtropical maze is named after the concentration of great cypresses found there, some of them more than 500 years old. The

FLAKY BARK *Flood waters inundate the stands of paperbark trees in Kakadu during the wet season.*

islands in the swamp, called hammocks, support oak trees, mahogany and gumbo limbo pines, dappled by orchids and brightly coloured butterflies.

SALTWATER LANDS

The Kakadu wilderness of the Northern Territory of Australia reveals the gradual shading between freshwater wetlands and the sea. In a plain beneath the jagged cliffs where the plateau of Arnhem Land comes to an abrupt end, freshwater rivers snake their way sluggishly through a green, sultry landscape to the sea. During the wet season from December to March, heavy rainfall replenishes the rivers and watering holes, but the region comes under increasing stress as the long dry season takes hold; almost no rain falls between May and October.

After the rains this is a landscape of unsurpassed beauty. Kingfishers dart over the swamps, perching in the shade of waterside groves where eucalyptus and the aptly named paperbark trees grow, while black-necked storks, known as jabirus, strut around on the

grassy lowlands. Deep pink giant water-lily blossoms break out of the mirror-still waters of the billabongs. This land is occupied by five Aboriginal clans including the Gagudju Aborigines (Kakadu is an imitation of their name). Their myths tell of a giant crocodile called Ginga who created the rocky margins of the wilderness where today thousands of rock paintings can be seen, some dating back 60 000 years. In reality there are two sorts of crocodile here, reflecting the dual nature of the land: the freshwater crocodile, and the larger saltwater crocodile

EXOTIC IMPORTS

Humans have introduced strange species to the Florida Everglades. The Australian melaleuca tree, imported for its supposed ability to drain land, is taking over large areas, earning itself the nickname, the 'Everglades Terminator'. Other imports include nine-banded armadillos from Mexico, which escaped from a travelling circus; rhesus monkeys imported by film crews making jungle movies; poisonous South American toads; and the Asian hydrilla weed, which can grow 1 ft (30 cm) a day and chokes the waterways.

which lives in the brackish estuaries and can reach lengths of up to 20 ft (6 m).

Salt marshes are protected from the full thrust of the tides by ridges of land, shingle or sand, or by mangrove forests. This is the meeting point where sluggish rivers and streams carrying silt-laden fresh water run into the salt water carried on the incoming tide. These are strange marginal worlds, best visited by boat, where only a select range of salt-tolerant plants – halophytes – can grow. Various types of plants are salt-tolerant – grasses, shrubs, succulents and others. There are also some unusual specialists such as the fleshy glasswort or samphire, with bulbous segments laden with salty fluid.

In temperate climates, salt marshes are dominated by sedges, rushes and grasses – such as eelgrass and spartina or cordgrass – the roots of which bind the loose, muddy soil into semistable banks and islands, which become ever firmer as layers of decaying

FRONTLINE MANGROVE *With their strong, arching roots, red mangroves usually form the vanguard along the coastline.*

bamboo forests of Maharashtra in India to the mangrove swamps of Bengal, in the Sunderbans region south-east of Calcutta. Tigers have excellent acceleration, but not much staying power over distance. The mangroves provide good cover for stalking, which tigers do mainly at night, pursuing

vegetation accumulate on them. Farther inland, tussocky banks develop, colonised by sea meadow grass, and by sea lavender, sea pinks and sea asters.

The marsh grasses provide a habitat for spiders, grasshoppers and mice, while the cycle of growth and decay of the grasses, broken down by bacteria and fungi, provides rich food sources for the fry and larvae in the water. Salt marshes are valuable spawning grounds for various species of shrimps, crabs and fish, which later move out to sea to complete their adult life. While in their infant stages, however, these abundant creatures provide a well-stocked larder for countless breeding birds, such as pelicans, plovers and herons.

MANGROVES ON THE MARCH

In tropical climates no plant can compete with the greatest coloniser among saltwater plants: the mangrove. In fact, over half of all tropical coastlines are lined by mangroves. Like an inverted candelabra, the arching, barnacle-encrusted roots straddle the mudflats, intertwining in dense webs to create robust defences against the sea.

Mangroves are on the march – a mangrove forest can advance by as much as 330 ft (100 m) a year. Mangrove seeds grow roots while on the tree, then, when ready, stab into the mud like javelins and take root

MANGROVE LIFE *An Indian tiger (right) takes to the water in the Sunderbans. Below: Nesting scarlet ibises bring flashes of colour to the Venezuelan coast.*

– or alternatively float off on the high tide in search of new lands to conquer.

In the tidal margins among the mangroves, pungent with sulphurous mud and salt-laden air, live some of the world's most remarkable creatures. Bug-eyed mudskippers – a half-way house between fish and amphibian, spending more than half their time out of water – scamper across the mud, and build elaborate mud castles as mating dens. Archer fish knock flying insects out of the air by spitting out well-aimed jets of water. The mangrove swamps of the Ganges Delta – the most extensive in the world – are one of the last refuges of the Indian tiger.

Throughout south and South-east Asia tigers – a natural enemy of mankind – have been increasingly restricted to reserves that hold out the prospect of saving them from extinction. In south Asia such reserves cover a broad range of habitats, from the

deer, monkeys, buffaloes, hogs, even rats and frogs. The Indian tiger is an impressive swimmer, happy to lunge into the limpid waters of the mangrove swamps in pursuit of its prey.

The mangroves are also invaded periodically by thousands of breeding birds – such as the 10 000 scarlet ibises of the Caroni Swamp of Trinidad, which annually convert the trees into a seething, squawking kaleidoscope of movement and colour.

RANK PROFUSION

Forests contain the greatest concentrations of living matter in the world. Ranging from California's towering redwood stands to the dense profusion of rain forests, many retain the mysterious, timeless qualities of their primeval forebears.

Rain falls on a high canopy of rain forest in the island of Martinique in the eastern Caribbean: billions of droplets on billions of leaves, each a tiny drum. The sound is soft but dense, like the blanket of electrical crackles from loudspeakers at rest, awaiting the explosion of sound. But in this case the crescendo is more measured. Droplets gather on the leaflets, gaining mass and bulk; they drip from tips and drum down on the larger leaves below – broad, deep green umbrellas designed to scoop up the weakened rays of sun that filter to the forest floor. The rain envelopes the forest with its sound and with its all-pervading, life-giving dampness.

By and large, though, this is a curiously still world. A land-based hermit crab stumbles across the path, then retreats into its borrowed shell. High above vast, arching bamboos, in the trees where trailing lianas begin, an unseen bird sings its plaintive call – just four notes of a strangely haunting chord. The warm air filters gently around the towering tree trunks. As night steals in, the heavy scents of the humus on the forest floor are released into the air, punctuated here and there by the pungent stench of a rotting fruit, or the fascinating perfume of a flower calling out for the attention of pollinating bats.

Dotted around the broad midriff of the world are thousands of rain forests – places where warmth and plentiful moisture sustain phenomenal levels of growth. As in wetlands, water is the key. Forests of all kinds need generous quantities of water. They need water to take in nutrients from the soil, and water for photosynthesis. Massive forests like that of the Amazon Basin are part of a self-generating cycle of water. By the process of transpiration, sap is drawn up through the plant from the roots, and moisture then evaporates through pores in the leaves and is released back into the atmosphere, eventually to be recycled as mist and rain.

FOREST CATHEDRALS

The coastal redwood forests of California are often compared with cathedrals. It is an apt metaphor. The bare trunks soar upwards like massive stone columns. The canopy lets in slanting rays of exquisitely dappled light, like the light that filters through stained glass, and the air is filled with a sweet woody smell, which recalls the gentlest, most subtle incense. In the early

MIGHTY COLUMNS *The foliage of sequoias (left) and redwoods is concentrated in the upper canopy (opposite), so that the impression from the ground is of a forest of columns.*

morning and in the evening, when the twilight is extended by the dense ranks of massive trunks, silver-grey mists soften the sounds still further, and smudge details of silhouettes. Out of sight from the ground, high up in the canopy are flying squirrels, red tree voles and nesting spotted owls. The marbled murrelet also nests in the high branches – a thrush-sized sea bird which spends its day searching for fish among the seastacks of the Californian coast.

The world's most massive living organism is the giant sequoia *(Sequoiadendron giganteum)* of California's high sierra. Sequoias can grow more than 300 feet (91 m) high, with diameters of over 100 ft (30 m). But sequoias are not the world's tallest trees. This accolade goes to their cousins, the coastal redwoods *(Sequoia sempervirens),* which can rise to nearly 370 ft (113 m), the equivalent of a 30-storey building. With diameters of up to 44 ft (13 m), redwoods can weigh 500 tons. Due to their weight and density, mature stands form the world's greatest biomass, (the total weight of all living things in a given area) an estimated 1780 tons per acre (720 tons per hectare) – over seven times that of a tropical rain forest.

Redwoods survive in a unique climatic pocket along the Californian coast, where

cool sea currents meet air warmed by the sun over the land to form thick summer fogs. At 85 in (2160 mm) per annum, rainfall is also moderately high, and the largest redwoods – such as those at the Humboldt Redwoods State Park – line the moist floors of river valleys. But it is the fog that sustains their huge bulk. It is thought that transpiration alone would not be enough to draw water from the roots to the tops of the trees, and so the upper canopy depends upon the moisture supplied by the mists. Indeed, there are three distinct microclimates in the redwood forest: one at the tree tops, where leaves are exposed to the heat of the sun and high levels of evaporation; another

LOGS OF STONE *The trees of the Petrified Forest National Park in Arizona died in the early part of the dinosaur age.*

OLD TIMERS *The bristlecone trees of California's White Mountains may be over 4500 years old, the oldest living trees.*

in the cooler lower level of the upper canopy, and a third on the dimly lit forest floor.

The redwoods themselves help to sustain their ecosystem. The huge amounts of evaporation exuded by each of the larger trees – some 500 gallons (1892 litres) a day – contribute to the evening mists and trap warmth in the forest. Few trees can compete with the redwoods in this environment. Douglas firs and Western hemlocks grow where they can, but the forest floor is mostly given over to low-lying plants such as lady ferns, sword and liquorice ferns, huckleberry, salmonberry, oxalis, and the shrublike poison oak – protected by an oil that is capable of causing a nasty skin rash.

When strong winds blow in from the coast, the forest becomes a place of howling fury. Since redwoods are surprisingly shallow-rooted, high winds are the cause of most tree deaths. When venerable giants topple, they often drag younger trees with them. Their place is soon taken by another generation, which start off as saplings growing from root outgrowths around the parent tree. (Although redwoods produce millions of seeds, only a small percentage of new trees grow from seed.) Because of their resistance to decay, the fallen logs may take several hundred years to rot away, during which time they become host to an estimated 700 species of fungi, 170 species of birds and mammals and 3200 species of insects.

ANCIENT TREES

Some coastal redwoods may live for 2000 years before they fall. The average age of the living 'old-growth' trees is 500-700 years. Since the 1850s, however, many have fallen victim to logging – so that now only pockets of them survive, mainly in national parks.

Not far from where they grow are the fossilised relics of forests that stood here in

WATER TOWERS *The trunks of Madagascan baobabs act as water reservoirs. Madagascar has six species of baobabs, in contrast to Africa's one.*

prehistoric times. The petrified forest near Calistoga has the remains of giant redwoods, while the Petrified Forest National Park in Arizona has trees from what was once a tropical marshland. These trees died some 225 million years ago. The decaying wood absorbed silica in the water and over the centuries was converted into agate.

The bristlecones of eastern California and Arizona are among the world's oldest living trees. Some may be more than 4500 years old. Their gnarled trunks have the appearance of stone, the result of the rigours of cold winters, very arid summers and the ravages of drought. Yet life is sustained by rivulets of bark which supply a lifeline to clusters of deep green needles on the strangely angular branches. Standing alone in areas of high desert or badlands, they strike strange, sculptural poses.

The baobabs, or boab trees, of Africa and north-west Australia have a similarly primeval air. Their huge, fleshy girths are crowned by

PANORAMA *A high point in the Alaskan taiga offers a glimpse over dense conifer forests to a lake and mountains beyond.*

MOOSE COUNTRY *A moose forages in the Alaskan taiga. Only the males carry the large, palm-shaped antlers.*

absurdly dainty branches and leaves. In contrast to the redwoods, when a baobab tree dies, its spongy wood rapidly disintegrates into a shapeless heap.

A NECKLACE OF TREES

Redwoods once grew across much of the Northern Hemisphere. They belonged to the landscape of the dinosaurs – and the mist-laden climate in which they survive is probably a replica of a more general climate in the age of the dinosaur.

Forests of a very different kind now grow where once the redwoods may have reigned supreme. Occupying the chilly latitudes to the south of the tundra, but to the north of the prairies and the steppes, is a vast ring of forest comprised mainly of pine, spruces and firs, but also of birch, alder and willow. The 'taiga', as this type of forest is called, is in fact the most extensive forest in the world, covering 11 per cent of the Earth's surface.

Taiga covers some of the most remote, uncharted parts of the world, known only to occasional loggers, prospectors or indigenous hunters and trappers, such as the Cree people of Quebec. Beneath the vast sky of the northern latitudes, the Quebec forest lies like a deep quilt across the rolling hills – and the forest covers the hills so densely from base to peak that distant views are rare and only glimpsed from rocky summits. Often the best views occur where the tree cover is broken by the many lakes that fill the valleys – but even here trees crowd in to the very edge of the rocky shoreline or gravel beaches. In autumn the deep greens of the conifers become a foil for the brilliant flashes of the maple leaves – yellow, deep red, russet and burnished gold. In winter, snow smothers the woodlands, turning them into a canvas of monochrome colour blocks: brilliant white and deep, dark shade.

Only certain plants are able to survive in the damp, often waterlogged soil of the taiga, and the rigorous conditions of the climate, where annual temperatures may vary by 100°C (180°F) between the brief summer and the bitterly cold depths of winter. Like steep-pitched roofs, conical conifer trees are designed to shed excessive weights of snow, while their waxy needles prevent evaporation and their thick resin resists freezing. The deciduous trees, by contrast, reduce their vulnerability to freezing temperatures by cutting the sap off from the leaves. As a result, the leaves lose their chlorophyll and transform into a cloak of radiant autumnal colours before dropping to the ground.

Animals of the taiga likewise have to be well adapted to the rigours of the seasons. Many are migratory visitors, such as caribou and moose, heading south out of the tundra and across the taiga as winter closes in. Clouds of flying insects, especially mosquitoes, must complete their adult life during the brief summer. Mammals, such as squirrels and lemmings, go into hibernation in winter, when their bodies achieve an almost death-like stillness – yet they are able to rouse themselves in extreme temperatures to prevent their organs from freezing. Brown bears, lynxes and wolves drift into long periods of slumber, but occasionally saunter out in search of food. Wolverines, the largest of the weasel family, have especially furry feet to help them run over the snow in pursuit of prey – which can include animals as large as deer.

One of the most significant animals of these regions is the beaver – the largest rodent of the Northern Hemisphere. Beavers, through their habit of building lodges and dams, have a dramatic impact on the landscape, altering the ecology of entire valleys.

The dams may be as much as 3000 ft (914 m) wide and house extended families of beavers. They use the lodges as refuges in winter, when they feed on stores of felled branches on the lake bottoms, beneath the ice.

KINGS AMONG FORESTS

The climatic conditions of the northern latitudes permit only brief spurts of growth. No such limitations apply to the world's tropical rain forests, where the seasons barely change at all. Some parts of the year are hot and wet, and others are even wetter. Trees and shrubs flower and fruit to their own rhythms, some at intervals of decades rather than years.

Much of life in a tropical rain forest takes place high in the upper canopies of the trees – an environment that has only recently been opened up to proper research through the use of suspended walkways. These upper branches are home to thousands of extraordinary animals and plants which, over the millennia, have developed fascinating ways

RAIN-FOREST WONDERS *A tree boa (below) coils round a banana flower. Leaf-cutter ants (below right) march off with burdens many times their body weight.*

THE WEIRD WORLD OF FUNGI

Some of the forests' strangest shapes, most fantastic colours, most fascinating textures, and most curious and pungent odours come from fungi. But what we see sprouting from the forest floor, or growing on damp, fallen logs, or climbing decaying tree trunks, are just the fruiting bodies of a complex organism that remains largely out of sight.

Lacking stems, roots and leaves, fungi are not plants at all – but in a class of their own. Networks of thread like filaments spread through the matter on which the fungus feeds, acquiring the carbohydrates which true plants manufacture through their chlorophyll. These networks of filaments can extend over huge areas: a honey fungus system growing in a forest in Michigan, USA, spreads over an area of 150 000 sq yd (125 400 m²), and may well be a single organism – the most extensive living thing on Earth. It is estimated to be 1500 years old.

PUFF OF SPORES *At the slightest knock, fungi puffballs send clouds of spores into the air.*

Mushrooms, toadstools and other fruiting bodies are thrown up to disperse the spores from which further fungi can grow; they have no need of pollination. Some of these are dispersed by insects or other animals, some are dropped from gills into the passing breezes, and others are catapulted into the air – as when a puffball bursts.

Fungi play a critical role in forests. They are one of the few organisms that can break down the cellulose and lignin in wood, and they accelerate the decay of fallen leaves. As a result, the nutrients contained in fallen leaves, branches and whole tree trunks can be released back into the soil and re-used by the trees. The distinctive smell of fungi, therefore, is not so much one of decay as one of regeneration.

---

of survival. Mammals, for instance, have a remarkable agility. In the Amazon rain forest, a number of species have highly sensitive finger-like pads on their prehensile tails which help them to move around. They include the howler, capuchin and woolly monkeys. In complete contrast, the three-toed sloth moves with mesmerising slowness. It hangs upside-down for virtually all its life: unusually, its hair grows backwards from the stomach to allow water to drain off it, and often acquires a green tinge of mould.

Because so much of life goes on high in the branches, or at night, and because most of its animals have highly tuned instincts to keep out of sight and harm's way, the rain forest may appear surprisingly deserted – even in a place like the Manú Biosphere Reserve in eastern Peru, which contains one of

continued on page 73

THREE FORESTS IN ONE

Basin can be a misleading term: rarely across its vast area does the Amazon Basin rise to a height of more than about 656 ft (200 m). It is less a basin than a vast plain, crossed by hundreds of sluggish rivers. These fill and flood during the rainy season – April to August to the north of the Equator, and December to June to the south. The height of the Amazon itself can vary by as much as 45 ft (13.5 m) – and all its tributaries regularly spill over their banks.

Plant growth in the Amazon Basin depends on two critical factors: competition for light and the availability of soil. As a result, there are three main kinds of forest in the basin. Tropical rain forest grows on the firmer, more elevated soil. Here competition for light pushes the tree canopy ever higher. The silk cotton, para nut and sucupira trees rise rapidly to 200 ft (61 m), leaving a dark interior of bare trunks and a sparsely covered forest floor starved of light.

Each level of altitude in this rain forest has its own ecosystem, from the sun-warmed 'emergent layer' of the treetops, to the dank forest floor, home to the termites, millipedes, beetles, crickets and mites which scurry around the leaf litter and assist the process of decay.

WET SEASON *After the rains, areas of várzea stay inundated for months. Only specialist plants tolerate such conditions.*

JUNGLE *The arched roots (below) of a guanandi tree (Symphonia globulifera) add to the tangle of plant life.*

ABOVE AND BELOW *Giant water-lily pads (above) crowd the still surface of the* igapós. *Beneath lurks an anableps fish (above right), ready to leap up to pluck insects and even hummingbirds out of the air.*

Wherever the canopy has collapsed, or cannot develop – on unstable river banks, for instance – a low tangle of shrubs, bushes, palms, bamboos, creepers and stunted trees develops. The result is a kind of storybook jungle – dense thickets of vegetation that can be penetrated only by hacking a path through it.

Large areas of the forest are flooded regularly or permanently. The trees that grow in seasonally flooded forest (*várzea*) have to be able to cope with unstable soil and long periods of sodden terrain. Various fish and animals swarm in with the flood, taking advantage of the nutrients which are released into the water by inundation. Permanently, or almost permanently, flooded forest (*igapós*) has its own specialist plants,

such as giant floating lilies, trees supported on buttressed roots; and animals which have adapted to a swampland existence, like the rare giant otter, freshwater sponges, the red-necked turtle, stingrays and electric eels capable of delivering a

shock of 500 volts. The anableps fish is equipped with an upper and lower retina in each eye which permits it to see simultaneously below and above water, so that it can pursue insects and even hummingbirds by leaping 6ft (1.8m) out of the water.

HARMLESS GUEST *Epiphytes feed off surface debris, not the host itself.*

THE TREE AS HOST

No tree stands alone: it is part of a complex ecosystem – home, dining room and resting place for hundreds of other species of plants and animals. The hospitality offered by trees is nowhere more generous than in a cloud forest, dampened almost permanently by low cloud or mist – like that of the Monteverde National Park in Costa Rica – where every branch of a single tree may be caked with thousands of other plants, such as lichens, mosses, bromeliads, ferns, vines, creepers, lianas and orchids.

Most of these are epiphytes: they use the tree as a perch only, but do not feed off it and harm it, as a parasitic plant would. Their roots take moisture from the air and find nutrients in debris in cracks in the bark. Nonetheless, these guests may not always be welcome: the sheer weight and density of the plants on a tree may well hinder its growth and affect its ability to compete for light.

Bromeliads create tiny worlds of their own high in the upper branches of cloud forest trees. The rosettes of some bromeliads trap water, creating miniature pools which attract a wide variety of creatures – insects, snakes, tree-climbing crabs, birds, monkeys and a host of small mammals – which come to drink and feed here. Dragonflies and mosquitoes may lay their eggs in the rosette. Some species of arrow-poison frogs give birth to their young on the forest floor. When the young reach tadpole stage, one or two climb on the father's or mother's back, and then the parent will climb high into a tree and deposit the tadpoles in the pool of water in a selected bromeliad rosette – to act as a miniature nursery until the tadpoles mature.

WORLDS WITHIN WORLDS
Frogs use the rosettes of bromeliads as nurseries for their tadpoles.

BRILLIANT COLOUR IN THE RAIN FOREST

The primary rule of the forest is eat or be eaten, and most animals have evolved with a mixture of habits and camouflage that allows them to survive by passing virtually unnoticed. Yet some fly in the face of this wisdom: instead of merging subtly into the background they stand out from it in all their glory.

Among the most richly coloured are the arrow-poison frogs of Central and South America. With splendidly evocative Latin names such as *Phyllobates terribilis* (so poisonous that it causes heart failure) and *Dendrobates fantasticus*, many of these species are exceptionally dangerous, and are used by rain-forest hunters to spike the tips of their poison arrows. The poison is exuded through the skin, making the frog dangerous even to touch. Their vivid colour acts as a warning to any predators: Danger! Do not approach!

However, over half the species of so-called arrow-poison frogs are not poisonous at all. They are using mimicry – exploiting the instinct that tells predators not to touch any frogs with this coloration.

The colours of some butterflies act as a kind of camouflage when they are moving through the speckled light of the rain-forest canopy. Many flowers in the canopy, by contrast, have bright colours in order to be seen, to lure birds and insects to their pollen through the dim light. For similar reasons many birds also have bright colours to attract mates, such as the spectacular male quetzal of Central America. Often these bright colours remain discreetly hidden beneath more sober feathers until mating time. The macaws of the Amazon Basin, however, have no such reticence. Three of the 16 South

POISON ALERT *The colouring of the arrow-poison frog is a visual warning to predators.*

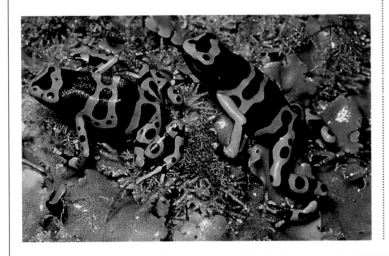

COLOUR FLASH *A red-and-green macaw and a blue-and-yellow macaw pose together.*

American species are named after their vivid primary colours: scarlet, red-and-green, and blue-and-yellow. Highly intelligent and large, powerful and numerous enough to survive predation, they have developed in open defiance of the usual evolutionary pressures to conform.

the richest concentrations of wildlife in the Amazon Basin. Spread out across its 7000 sq miles (18 130 km²) are colonies of raucous howler monkeys, night-prowling jaguars and ocelots, pig-like peccaries, 15 ft (4.6 m) long caimans, giant jabiru storks, katydid insects that look almost identical to a leaf, and numerous chirruping tree frogs. Leaf-cutting ants march in columns along logs, bearing cut fragments of leaves to their nests; there, other grades of ants chew up the leaves and then, in labyrinthine underground chambers, farm fungi on the debris, from which the colony feeds.

FOREST DIVERSITY

Rain forests contain the greatest diversity and concentrations of plant and animal life in the world. The statistics are enough to send the mind reeling – and we are still counting. The Amazon Basin alone contains a third of all of the world's animal species. It has 100 000 species of plants: Europe has 12 000. An acre (0.4 ha) of rain forest will contain some 80 species of tree: a European deciduous forest will contain half a dozen. About 90 000 species of fungi are found in tropical rain forests – out of a

SWALLOW A PIG WHOLE

The world's largest snake lives in the forest swamps of the Amazon Basin. Anacondas reach lengths of up to 33 ft (10 m). They kill their prey by constricting – winding their body around the victim and squeezing the breath out of it or causing heart failure. They usually prey on tapirs, deer, capybaras, water birds, and domesticated animals. Like all snakes they swallow their prey whole, head first. Their digestive juices are powerful enough to break down the food, but may take weeks to do so.

world total of 100 000. It is estimated that 25 per cent of drugs used in modern medicine are based on ingredients that come from tropical forests.

All rain forests have their own rich ecosystems. Those of New Guinea have no primates, pigs or deer but instead support some of the most fascinating animals of all the rain forests. Deep in the forests that cloak the steep and ragged inland hills and mountains, male birds of paradise perform elaborate courtships with fabulous tail feathers, while bower birds build fantastic nests of feathers, pebbles, shells, flowers and fruit to attract a mate. The world's largest butterfly lives in Papua New Guinea – the Queen Alexandra's birdwing, with a wingspan of almost 1 ft (30 cm). Sugar gliders sail with outstretched limbs between the branches of the tall araucaria and rosewood trees, in search of sap and gum to feed on.

The Ndoki rain forest of the Congo is home to giant swallowtail butterflies, hornbills, colobus monkeys, snub-nosed pottos, mandrills, leopards, okapis and lowland gorillas, as well as plentiful leeches, tsetse flies and ticks. There are also little-studied herds of forest elephants, which, in response

to their habitat, have evolved as smaller versions of their grassland cousins.

The dense growth of the rain forest – the huge girths of brazil nut and cotton trees, and the thickness of the canopy that blocks out almost all direct sunlight – suggests robust ecosystems. In fact, rain forests are very fragile environments. The soil is poor – a shallow layer of topsoil, which is comparatively low in nutrients. But the trees of the rain forest are remarkably efficient at recycling the nutrients of decaying vegetation, assisted by fungi, insects and the digestive systems of thousands of species of animals. Once the trees have gone, the nutrients become rapidly depleted. Farming on clear-cut tropical forest is usually sustainable for just a couple of years before the soil becomes barren. A single brazil nut tree, by contrast, can provide far more nutrition for humans than any agricultural crop grown in the soil beneath its spread.

FOREST OF BEARDS

Much less known than tropical rain forests are the rain forests of temperate climate zones. In certain places, heavy rainfall or thick mists throughout the year, and a cool,

FAIRY-TALE FOREST *Festoons of club moss drape the branches of a big leaf maple tree in the Hoh temperate rain forest.*

moderate climate with mild winters, will produce extraordinary damp wonderlands, where plant growth is as abundant as any tropical forest. Such rain forests are found only in rare pockets around the world, such as Milford Sound in southern New Zealand, and on the island of Yaku-Shima in Japan. Another is the Hoh rain forest of the Olympic National Park in western Washington State, USA.

The Hoh rain forest receives around 150 in (3810 mm) of rain a year, caused by precipitation from moisture-laden air rising rapidly from the coast and up the flanks of Mount Olympus. Many of the trees – such as Douglas firs, Western hemlocks, Sitka spruce and red alders – grow to record heights in these conditions.

The forest floor here is so densely covered with ferns, oxalis and horsetails that young trees cannot compete. Many of the successful Sitka spruce and Western hemlock saplings begin life where seeds have

settled on a fallen log, raised above the tangle of the forest floor. They take moisture and nutrients from the bark and rotting wood of the decaying log (known as the 'nurse log') until their roots can reach down to the soil beneath. The result is that mature trees grow along the line of the nurse log, their ever-stronger roots arching over the log. Eventually the nurse log rots away completely, leaving a row of trees with their trunks suspended above the ground on bandy-legged constructions of arched roots.

PROLIFERATION BY THE MILLIONS

Forests rarely do anything by halves. Female lemmings in the taiga produce litters of some eight young three times every year. They can mate just 19 days after their own birth and produce their first litter 20 days later. Termite queens lay more than 1000 eggs a day. Army ants march by night in columns half a million strong, 30 ft (9 m) across, destroying anything in their path.

One of the most bizarre manifestations of forest profusion occurs in the isolation of Christmas Island, a tiny Australian territory south of Java. Every year in late October or November, around the time of a new moon, 120 million red crabs emerge from their moist burrows in the rain forest and head for the coast to breed, a perilous journey that lasts between one and three weeks. The males begin the exodus, followed by the females, which, after mating at the coast, will each produce 100 000 eggs, depositing them in the shallow waters of the sea before heading inland. Several weeks later more millions of young will emerge from the sea to join the adults in the rain forest.

During this period the island is awash with red crabs. They swarm over the roads, puncturing car tires; they invade the golf course, kitchens, shops and garages. They paint the sea cliffs red with thousands of densely packed shells. Local people put up with this surreal experience. The usual evolutionary checks and balances might have come into play if the red crabs had any major predators besides herons and robber crabs. But even the world's most voracious predator has little use for them: the red crab is considered unpalatable by humans.

AGAINST THE ODDS

3

DESERT FLOWER *A camomile plant flowers within days of rain in the Arabian desert.*

LACK OF RAINFALL MEANS LACK OF LIFE. THERE ARE PLACES ON EARTH WHERE VIRTUALLY NO RAIN OR ANY OTHER FORM OF PRECIPITATION FALLS. SOME ARE SEARINGLY HOT DESERTS; OTHERS ARE ARID LANDS RAKED BY BITTER WINTERS. OTHERS STILL ARE THE ICE-BOUND POLAR REGIONS. SUCH ENVIRONMENTS OFFER PRECIOUS LITTLE ASSISTANCE TO LIFE, AND YET A SURPRISING NUMBER OF TENACIOUS PLANTS AND ANIMALS HAVE EVOLVED FINELY TUNED STRATEGIES TO ALLOW THEM TO SURVIVE IN SPECIALIST NICHES. THIS SAME TENACITY CAN ALSO BE SEEN IN THE WAY PLANTS AND ANIMALS QUICKLY RECOLONISE LANDSCAPES THAT HAVE BEEN DEVASTATED BY NATURAL DISASTER.

RAW LANDSCAPE *Ice creates a savage beauty in Greenland.*

THE WORLD'S FRYING PAN

In hot deserts, rocks crack in the heat, sandstorms strip the paint off cars, and a human heart may collapse under the strain of pumping thickened blood around the body. Yet shrimps and paper-thin poppies survive in this hostile world.

For thousands of years, the wind has torn at the granite rocks of the Ahaggar Mountains of southern Algeria, shaping them into a bizarre jumble of contorted forms – wedding cakes and spires, arches and humanoid sculptures. By day surface temperatures rise to 85°C (185°F); by night temperatures may drop to freezing as the heat, unhindered by clouds, escapes upwards into the atmosphere. Occasional loud bangs are heard, like the report of a gun, as rocks crack under the stress of this thermal roller-coaster. Now and again, violent downpours slake the dry rock, causing the surface to become weak and friable. Then the desert wind races through the chasms, carrying with it a stinging belt of corrosive sand, which rubs away at the pedestals of rock.

This is a sand desert in the making, the relentless abrasion of rock into its smallest components very gradually reducing mountains to dust. The intermediate stages create some of the most spectacular of all desert

and semidesert landscapes, at Ahaggar, at Tassili N'Ajjer near-by – or among the sandstone sculptures of the Arches of Utah in the USA and Monument Valley on the Utah–Arizona border to the south.

To the north of the Ahaggar Mountains lie what they will become: great seas of drifting sand. Called *erg* in Arabic, the sand deserts are at once majestic and terrifying. In the dry air, breezes scurry over the Grand Erg of Algeria, piling up the sand into vast, soft heaps. From the shifting valleys beneath the

WIND POWER *A precariously balanced rock in the Ahaggar region of southern Algeria demonstrates the corrosive effect of wind and sand.*

dunes, it may be tempting to mount to the crests, but the sand is so soft that walking up the flanks is exhausting. From the summit all that is visible is a maze of further dunes stretching in all directions. There are no other landmarks or fixed points – except for rare oases. Like a sea, the erg is constantly on the move, subtly changing in the winds and breeze, every now and then invading and overwhelming an oasis, just as the sea will erode a shoreline and flood the interior.

Deserts are defined by their lack of water, and some authorities put a figure on it. They say that anywhere that receives less than 10 in (254 mm) of rain in a year is a desert. Hence the rocky Ahaggar Mountains qualify as desert as well as the rolling sand dunes at their feet. In fact, despite the traditional image of deserts as seas of sand, less than a third of the world's deserts are covered by dunes. More common are the flat pavements of rock and stones called by their Arabic name *reg*. Deserts in Australia known

PARCHED LANDS *Cold coastal currents deprive the Namib Desert of moisture. Here an acacia tree has succumbed to the ebb and flow of drought.*

as 'gibber deserts', from a native Aboriginal word, are a variation of this, speckled by millions of small, wind-polished stones. The gibber desert west of Lake Eyre in Australia has been scoured by the wind, which long ago effaced all the contours of the land, and is now scratching at its base elements, a scattering of rocks separated by the agents of their erosion – granules of gravel and sand. This is the landscape of despair – endless, without reprieve, foot-jarring.

ARID BEAUTY

The deserts of the world fit into two broad bands around the globe centred roughly on the tropics of Cancer and Capricorn. These are zones of low precipitation. Warm air

SAND RIPPLES *Winds blowing consistently from the same direction create ripple effects in Australia's Simpson Desert (above) and New Mexico's White Sands Desert (left).*

admiration and awe. Yet these are treacherous and misleading landscapes – extremely dangerous to human beings who do not know precisely what they are doing. The human body will exude up to 21 pints (12 litres) of sweat in a day in the scorching temperatures of the open desert. This has to be replaced, otherwise the blood thickens and overloads the heart. Human skin is easily burnt by the sun, and sweating – a natural way to regulate body temperature through the cooling effect of evaporation – becomes fatally hindered if the pores of the skin are damaged by sunburn.

The weather can be ugly and unpredictable. Wind storms launch a carpet of moving sand across the desert floor and send clouds of choking dust to a height of 10 000 ft (3048 m), affecting the weather in regions far beyond. Dust from the Sahara occasionally falls on London. Deserts may have an average rainfall of 10 in (254 mm) or less – but the entire quota for a decade may fall in just an hour. Such downpours cause erratic and devastating flooding, capable of pushing boulders and trees before it. At other times thirst-quenching rain falls – but evaporates in the heat before it reaches the ground.

Of all the desert environments none is more majestic or threatening than a sea of sand dunes. The Grand Erg of Bilma in the Ténéré Desert of Niger is an example, a vast sea of dunes 750 miles (1200 km) wide. The world's largest sand desert is known simply as Rub al-Khali, the Empty Quarter, and covers much of the southern part of the Arabian Peninsula. In the Simpson Desert in central Australia, iron oxide particles have turned the sand red, contrasting vividly with the blue skies. The dazzling White Sand Desert of New Mexico is composed of fine gypsum.

The lightest breeze sends grains of sand trickling over the ridges and summits of the dunes, gradually altering their shape and

rises at the Equator and circulates towards the nearest pole. However, by the time it reaches the tropics it has released most of its moisture. Local conditions also come into play. Rain-shadow deserts, such as the Mojave Desert of the American West, occur in the shadow of mountains. The mountains force air on the prevailing breezes to rise and deposit its moisture, depriving the land beyond of rain. Coastal deserts, such as the Namib Desert of southern Africa, occur where cold ocean currents, accompanied by cold air with little moisture, brush against the land. The Atacama Desert of northern Chile is both a rain-shadow desert, deprived of rain by the Andes, and a coastal desert thanks to the cold Peru Current. It is the driest place on Earth, with less than 1 in (25 mm) of rain per annum. Parts of it have not received rain since historical records began.

Another group of deserts, continental deserts, lie so far inland that virtually all precipitation is exhausted by the time it reaches them. The Gobi Desert of Mongolia and northern China is the classic example of this. Although generally referred to as a cold desert because of its bitterly cold winters, it is also extremely hot in summer, when temperatures can rise to 45°C (113°F).

Dry and inhospitable as they are, many deserts are famed for their own kind of austere beauty. The vast spaces; the clear, dry air; the savagery of the landscape tempered by the delicate shades of pastel colours – all have their own allure which invites both

NAMIB WAYS *A darkling 'head-stander' beetle (above right) catches fog-borne moisture. The Aporosaura lizard (above left) keeps only two feet at a time on the burning sand.*

even their whole position. The nature of the prevailing winds sculpts the sand into characteristic forms – crescent-shaped *barchans*, star-shapes or ripples called *seifs*. The largest dunes can reach heights of 820 ft (250 m).

All life forms have difficulty in coping with the arid conditions of the desert, but sand presents the greatest problems. Plants cannot take root in this dry, shifting terrain, and few animals survive happily in such a soft, shadeless world.

LIVING OFF THE CLOUDS

Yet even among the sand dunes there is life. Lining the coast of Namibia is a deep band of dunes stretching 1300 miles (2100 km) and forming the western margin of the Namib Desert. Beetles and other small insects scurry across the sand, scavenging tiny bits of plant debris and animal waste that blow in on the wind from more fertile zones on the periphery of the desert, or from plant growth that springs up temporarily in

narrow gravel valleys between the dunes after periodic rain showers. Many of these insects bury themselves in the sand when the daytime heat becomes too intense. Here, though, they may fall prey to legless sand skinks, eel-like lizards that 'swim' through the soft sand by wriggling their bodies. Legs are a hindrance when moving like this, and so the skinks have lost all but a remnant of them. Meanwhile, on the hot ground, the

Aporosaura lizard uses another technique to avoid contact with the surface. It balances on two feet, holding up the other two to cool in the air. Each form of wildlife has evolved adaptations to cope with the problems this merciless environment presents.

The most curious aspect of the Namib Desert is its climate. The desert is a product of the cold Benguela Current that sweeps up the shore of south-western Africa from

A CHANGE IN THE WEATHER

In the heart of the Sahara Desert in southern Algeria lies one of its most unforgiving environments, a landscape of wind-tortured rocks and canyons called Tassili N'Ajjer. Set on a plateau rising to 7395 ft (2254 m), it contains an extraordinary art gallery – thousands of rock paintings and engravings, made over a period of some 6000 years, from about 6000 BC to 100 BC.

These give an account of the region's climatic history. The earliest show elephants, hippos, rhinos, giraffes, cattle, gazelles and fish, pointing to a climate that was much wetter than today's. Hunters appear among the animals, but later

paintings from around 4000 BC show cattle herders, indicating a pastoral way of life. By 1200 BC there are images of chariots, suggesting contact with Mediterranean cultures. In the last phase there are paintings of camels – the essential vehicle for a landscape that had degenerated into a desert dotted with oases.

FERTILE TIMES *A rock painting from Tassili N'Ajjer shows herders with their cattle.*

This is evidence that the Sahara was not always a desert, and probably underwent a radical change after the end of the last Ice Age about 10 000 years ago. Highland regions, however, may have resisted the process by providing pockets of wetter climate that sustained a broader variety of life. Just 500 miles (800 km) south of Tassili N'Ajjer lie the Aïr Mountains of Niger. Rising to 6400 ft (1950 m), they still provide an isolated refuge for gazelles, ostriches, antelopes and baboons – and here, too, are rock paintings of elephants and giraffes dating back some 5000 years.

THE DESERT IN BLOOM

If tropical forests reveal nature the great showman, the desert reveals its talents as the master of grand illusion. Quite suddenly, almost overnight, a bleak and arid desert can be transformed into a lush-looking pastureland of startling beauty, covered with delicate and brilliantly coloured wild flowers.

This transformation occurs after rainfall. Rain may be a rare, isolated occurrence, but on the surface of the desert there are thousands of seeds that have been waiting for this opportunity. After rain they burst into life with remarkable speed, and grasses and numerous flowering plants such as poppies, daisies and desert primroses turn the landscape into a bejewelled carpet of green.

These plants have to complete their cycle of life and produce new seeds before the water dries up – and many do so within three weeks. Then they die away again and the desert returns to its arid emptiness. Because of the short and unpredictable span of their growing life, these plants are known as ephemerals.

A real threat to the survival of ephemerals is a short burst of rain which triggers germination but is not enough to sustain the plant's full life cycle. To avoid the dangers of such false starts, many ephemerals have

FLORAL TRIBUTE *Sturt's desert pea is named after the 19th-century explorer of Australia, Charles Sturt.*

evolved seeds coated with a waxy layer. Only when this layer is fully immersed in water, and enough water is ensured, will it dissolve and allow germination to begin.

Such flourishes of plant life in the desert may be isolated, but they

QUICK RESPONSE *Seeds lying dormant in the Sahara start germinating within hours of a rain shower.*

DESERT COLOUR *Poached egg daisies and purple parakeelya flowers pop up from the desert sand of central Australia.*

occur often enough over a large area for the nomadic herdsmen of North Africa and the Middle East to know their patterns. They can read the clouds well enough to seek out these patches of temporary pasture, and will make haste to follow them.

Antarctica. The cold air, however, causes the warm desert air to condense, and during the night thick banks of fog roll in from the coast, bathing the landscape with precious airborne droplets of moisture.

The 'head-stander' beetle makes use of this in a remarkable way. Groups of the beetles climb to the dune ridges at dawn and stand with their rear ends raised to the incoming breezes. Moisture from the fog condenses on their backs and then drips down their bodies to their mouths.

CAREFUL USERS ONLY

Desert plants use various survival strategies. Some are perennials that sit out the desert heat and use whatever water becomes available with great frugality. Many of these have waxy surfaces that reduce water loss caused by evaporation. The pebble plants of the Namib Desert are so compact they look like stones – until they produce lavish flowers. They have tough, leathery surfaces that hold in their stores of moisture, and make it hard for animals to plunder them.

By contrast, kokerboom, or quiver trees, in the Namib Desert set their spiky leaves

SURVIVAL SKILLS *The Namib Desert's kokerboom (quiver tree) holds its leaves high, to reach cooler air.*

20 ft (6 m) above the baking ground, on branches dusted with silvery powder to reflect the sunlight, while the bizarre-looking halfmens sport an unkempt coiffure of seaweed-like leaves on top of a tall column coated with protective spines.

The supreme desert plant is the cactus. Virtually all cacti come originally from the New World – although elsewhere the huge and varied Euphorbia plant family has developed cactus-like species which have many features in common with true cacti.

Desert cacti are streamlined for survival. They have extensive root networks, which spread out beneath the surface of the desert, ready to absorb as much water as possible after rains. This is stored in fibrous stems. The characteristic concertina shape of many cacti, such as the Golden Barrel (*Echinocactus grusonii*), is designed to expand and contract according to the amount of water stored. Cacti tend to have vertical shapes and thick, waxy skins which minimise the

THE OLDEST LIVING PLANTS?

Creosote bushes in the deserts of south-western North America are named after the creosote-like smell of their resinous leaves. This is no accident. The toxic sap of the creosote bush acts as a deterrent – to both animals and other plants. The extensive root network prevents most other plants from competing. The bushes tend to spread outwards from a central point and form rings up to 80 ft (25 m) across. Although their leaves and branches are constantly renewed, some may have been growing for 12 000 years.

impact of sunlight, reflect away its rays and prevent water loss through evaporation.

As natural water barrels, cacti attract all kinds of thirsty animals. To fend them off, they have evolved spines – in fact, modified leaves – as their prime means of defence,

SAFE HAVEN *A Gila woodpecker searches for grubs on a saguaro. The birds also sometimes dig hollows in saguaros for nests.*

and these are very effective in discouraging animals from risking their tender mouths and limbs to pillage a cactus's moisture. Even the softer white hairs of the cacti called *senilis*, such as *Cephalocereus senilis* or 'old man cactus', make good deterrents.

Cacti reproduce by several methods. New cacti spring up from roots and stems. Some, such as the cholla 'jumping' cactus, readily release segments onto the fur of passing animals, so their offspring will be distributed far and wide. Sexual reproduction requires pollination, which usually means attracting insects, the most common animals in the desert. But because of the scale of the desert, cacti need to send out strong beacons to attract pollinators. These come in the form of short-lived and short-stalked but spectacular flowers.

King of all the cacti is the saguaro – the magnificent giant that grows only in the Sonoran Desert of the south-western USA and Mexican borderlands. A saguaro can grow to a colossal 52 ft (16 m), and live for 200 years. The poisonous sap and spines

deter most animals from plundering its store of water, but Gila woodpeckers and screech owls will often brave this peril and use a hole in a saguaro to make a nest. A saguaro grows first as a single column, and will develop its curious limbs only after they reach a height of 16 ft (5 m). Groups of saguaros make an arresting sight. Standing silently in their evenly distributed ranks, they strike distinctive poses that have often been compared with comical human characters – the traffic policeman, the gunslinger, the drunk.

WATER CARRIER *A male Saharan spotted sand grouse collects water for his chicks in his breast feathers.*

The careful use of water is essential to all desert plants. Some, like cacti and succulents, store it in their stems; others store it in bulbs or tubers. Others still, such as grasses, have wide networks of roots which stretch out beneath the surface of the desert, ready to take up the maximum amount of water dropped by a rain shower before it evaporates. Yet others, such as tamarisks, have very long roots which reach down to groundwater that lies far beneath the surface.

There are other plants in the desert which are not perennials. They grow, flower and produce new seeds in a very short season after rains. In temperate climates they would be called annuals – but in the desert they do not follow such a regular calendar and instead are called ephemerals. Their seeds may lie dormant for long periods of time before a burst of rain sends them into a flurry of activity as they race to produce more seeds before the water disappears.

STRATEGIES FOR SURVIVAL

Animals of the desert use strategies that mirror those of plants, the most important of which is the conservation of water. Most desert animals obtain all the water they need from their food – whether plants or other animals. They do not need to drink at all,

and they lose little water from sweating or defecating. Insects such as ants, locusts and beetles, and arachnids such as scorpions, spiders and huge solifuge camel 'spiders' have waxy skins that hold in the moisture.

Heat avoidance is important. Tiny slivers of shade, in rock crevices or beneath the overhang of larger rocks, create microclimates that offer critical differences in temperature. Reptiles take on the heat of their surroundings, and have to be warm in order to be active. But even they cannot afford to raise their body temperatures above 48°C (118°F) and must avoid the soaring temperatures of the middle of the day by taking shelter. Like the majority of desert animals, they are most active at the end of the day, and because the surface of the desert remains warm, they remain active well after dark.

Others animals, such as the gerbils and fennec foxes of the Sahara, or the meerkats of the Kalahari, spend most of the daylight hours in their burrows, where the temperature remains

BIDING TIME *The eggs of North American tadpole shrimps survive drought and heat to come to life after rain.*

several degrees lower than at the surface. Larger mammals, such as the dama gazelle, cannot do this. Instead they remain very still during the heat of the day, avoiding the muscular activity that generates heat and risks water loss.

Mammals have to keep their body temperature more or less constant. Panting and sweating help them to do this. The fennec fox and the American jack rabbit also have outsize ears which help to radiate heat and cool the blood passing through them.

Birds have an easier time in the desert. With the exception of owls and nightjars, they are mainly active by day. Their feathers act as insulation against the heat and they are able to seek out the cooler air of higher altitudes, from which they can spot any temporary patches of green or water.

STONY FACED *When still, the stone grasshopper of the Namib Desert is indistinguishable from its background.*

Several birds remain in the desert through much of the year, and even breed there. In the desert a parent bird often needs to sit on its eggs, not to keep them warm but cool – only the thick, enamel-like shell of an ostrich egg is able to survive the full blast of the sun unshaded. The white-crowned black wheatear builds its nest on a loosely constructed pile of pebbles which provides a form of ventilation. The sand grouse has adopted a cunning way of collecting water for its young. The male flies off to find water perhaps 20 miles (32 km) away, and gathers droplets in his chest feathers, which he carries back to the nest.

Like most desert animals, the sand grouse is buff-coloured. Its speckled feathers are extremely difficult to pick out from the gravel surfaces where it likes to nest. Camouflage is a vital feature of survival in a place where there are so few plants and where so many animals live by hunting.

To assist in their hunting, and for their protection, several desert animals are equipped with powerful poisons. Some scorpions are armed with highly toxic nerve poisons, while the North American desert has one of the world's very few venomous lizards – the Gila monster. Growing to 20 in (51 cm), this strange-looking, scaly, black-and-yellow creature feeds on other lizards, insects and small rodents.

A few desert animals survive long bouts of drought and intense heat by 'estivation', the warm-weather equivalent of hibernation, slowing down their metabolisms to induce a sleep-like torpor. Some snails in the Sahara are known to become dormant for eight years, while the spadefoot toad of the North American desert buries itself in the mud after rain, envelopes itself in mucus and settles down for a long wait. After the next rain it emerges from its hiding place, mates and produces eggs in little more than 24 hours.

BUSHMEN — DESERT SURVIVORS

For 25000 years, the Bushmen of the Kalahari Desert have practised the art of survival, and – with the exception of the Australian Aborigines – no people on Earth have a better understanding of the desert. Those bushmen who still live as hunter-gatherers in the Kalahari survive in conditions where other humans would fail. They have an intimate knowledge of water sources, and when these become scarce they find water in plants, such as lily bulbs, wild melons and the cactus-like Sansevieria. They also exploit pockets of moisture by creating sip wells. Digging into damp sand, they extract tiny quantities of water by sucking it up through a grass straw, and then they store it in an empty ostrich shell.

Much of the Bushmen's moisture intake comes from their normal diet – from meat hunted by the men with poison-tipped arrows, or the plants foraged by the women, which include the nutritious marama bean.

The San, as Bushmen call themselves, were the original inhabitants of southern Africa before being pushed off the better land by migrating cattle herders from the north around 500 years ago. Today there are only about 55000 left and fewer than 2000 live as hunter-gatherers in the desert.

NATURAL FLASKS *The tough shells of ostrich eggs make handy water containers.*

These eggs then become tadpoles within another day – pursuing a fast-forward progression to adulthood while the water lasts.

To target desert rainwater successfully, both plants and animals tend either to fix their aim precisely at where they have succeeded before – or to scatter their options as widely as possible. Rather like the seeds of ephemeral plants, the eggs of some animals may lie dormant in the sand for many years, either in shallow scoops where rain is likely to settle, should it fall, or blown about in the wind and strewn haphazardly across wide areas of the desert floor. Then, after rain, they spring into life, and make a desperate bid to complete their life cycle and reproduce – in less than a week in the case of mosquitoes – before the water dries up. This is how puddles which collect after rain – for example, in shallow bowls among the rocks in the midst of the Utah desert – are found to be alive with insect larvae, fairy shrimps and tadpoles, feeding on algae and each other. Despite a temperature range that varies between freezing and 65°C (150°F), the eggs survive in the sand. No one knows for sure how long they remain viable – possibly for hundreds of years.

FUTURE ZONE

Some 5000 years ago the Thar desert on the border between Pakistan and India supported a large agricultural population; now it is a wasteland. Over time, desert margins drift in and out of fertility, sometimes well-watered and green, sometimes semidesert. In this century, however, deserts are growing fast – estimated by some at about 40 sq miles (104 km²) a day. The Sahel, a band of semidesert across Africa south of the Sahara, reveals the consequences of a cycle of growing aridity, increasing population pressures and a resulting strain on resources. Semidesert, capable of supporting finely tuned agriculture, becomes desert capable of supporting only highly specialised animals, among which humankind – especially modern humankind – does not number.

HAVENS OF GREEN

Set amidst the merciless environment of the desert, oases are islands of fertility where plants and animals have all the water they need to survive and flourish. They are the exceptions that prove the harsh rules of desert life.

The beauty of the colour green takes on a new meaning in the desert. Here is life, water, sustenance, shade and hope. Beyond it lies hardship, danger, despair and death. Nowadays, cars, trucks and buses travel swiftly on paved roads across the world's deserts and, as a result, the preciousness of oases has been somewhat eroded. Yet even with the wonders of modern technologies, the knife-edge conditions that allow an oasis to survive or fail remain as critical and delicate as ever.

Deserts are littered with the haunting reminders of failure – oases where the water ran dry, where their finely tuned irrigation systems were disrupted by strife or overpopulation or invasion by sand, where trade collapsed as new routes evolved. The desert soon reclaims these ghost towns, overwhelming them with sand, scattering their constituent parts and grinding them into dust.

Despite the appearances, there is plenty of water in the desert. The bulk of it is underground, however, and too deep to reach. Oases are places where there is enough accessible water to make the land consistently fertile. Some oases are tiny – just a few bushes and

FERTILE POCKETS *Water in the Sahara Desert is often signalled by tough, tolerant and resilient date palms.*

GROUND WATER AND WELLS

There are millions of gallons of water lying beneath most deserts. Some is water that has travelled through permeable strata of rock, perhaps down inclines that stretch hundreds of miles from distant hills and mountains where rainfall or snow is regular and heavy. But much of it is fossil water: it has been there for many thousands of years, lying trapped in aquifers, water-bearing strata of rock, sealed by a layer of impermeable rock.

By some estimates there is enough water under the Sahara to supply 150 million people for 500 years. Certainly, in principle, it would be possible to supply many more oases with water by exploiting untapped ground water. However, there are three problems. Can the water be reached? Can it be extracted economically? Will the supply last?

Most oases rely on non-fossil sources of water – water sources that are replenished by annual rainfall in distant hills and mountains. Some centre upon springs, at which water issues from the incline of the permeable rock layer. In certain circumstances, pressure in the aquifer may make the water gush out at the surface as an artesian well. But most oases are in depressions – where the land surface drops closest

WATER PRESSURE *Water gushes from an artesian well.*

ANIMAL STRENGTH *Water buffaloes and other animals are still used to raise water in parts of Egypt.*

to the ground water. The water may appear at the surface as pools, but usually a well has to be sunk to reach it. These days the position of accessible sources of water beneath the ground can usually be pinpointed by geological analysis.

Water can be drawn up the well by buckets or pumped up mechanically. The deeper the well, the more likely it is that a machine will be used. But mechanical pumps are expensive to run. Fossil ground water is often too deep to extract economically. It costs too much to sink the well, and too much to run and maintain the pumps. Besides this, it is not a renewable resource: it will eventually run out.

palm trees surrounding a brackish spring. Others are vast, supporting tens of thousands of people. Biskra in Algeria, an oasis known to the Romans as Vescera and famous for its thousands of date palms, is today an important commercial and administrative centre with a population close to 100 000 people.

Most desert soil is potentially fertile, rich in nutrients and minerals. With the careful use of water, it can be coaxed into producing a range of fruit, vegetables and grain – such as wheat, millet, onions, tomatoes, peas, eggplants, melons, citrus, peaches, pomegranates, apples, pears, olives, grapes and tobacco. And then there are the dates.

According to an Arab legend, after Allah created the Earth he had two lumps of clay left over: with one he created the camel and with the other the date palm. The date palm is the quintessential oasis plant. Given enough water – and a date palm consumes large quantities of it, though it does tolerate brackish water – it will grow rapidly and

WATERING THE LAND   *Channels bring water to neat, oblong patches of worked soil in an oasis in Morocco (left). Fodder grass is grown beneath the shade of date palm in a Tunisian oasis (below).*

produce abundant fruit, as much as 200 lb (90 kg) a year. In traditional oasis life, date palms are cherished not simply for their fruit. The fronds are used to make roofing, mats and baskets; sugar is made from the sap. The trunks are used as timber for building; fibres are used to make rope, nets and sacking. The stalks on which the dates grow are made into brushes, and the seeds can be ground up to make a coffee-like drink.

THE PRICE OF WATER

The key to oasis dwelling is water management. Water sometimes appears in pools on the surface. But these circumstances are rare. More likely, the water will be raised or pumped to the surface via wells which reach down to ground water. Alternatively, the water

THE EFFECTS OF EVAPORATION

The climate is the biggest enemy of oasis agriculture. The heat of the sun causes rapid evaporation. This can mean that out of 6 gallons (27 litres) of water delivered to crops, only one will be used by the plants. The rest will vanish into the air.

One of the most damaging effects of this evaporation is the buildup of mineral salts in the soil. All water carries minerals, but when it evaporates it leaves the minerals behind. The salinity which results damages plants, preventing their roots from taking up water and nutrients effectively. Good soil drainage goes some way to preventing the buildup of salts, but desert soil tends to drain poorly. Countless bold new irrigation schemes have been made useless by the blight of salinity.

Various techniques have been developed in recent years to make the delivery of water to plants more

efficient. These include trickle or drip irrigation, which delivers small but constant quantities of water to the plants' roots, and the use of plastic as mulches and 'polytunnels', which prevents moisture from escaping. These have been very successful in Israel, but require a great deal of

capital and technical investment, which is often beyond the reach of many of the poorer countries faced with desert conditions.

MINIMUM WASTE *Crops grown in plastic tunnels in Israel are irrigated using the drip system.*

may be brought in from afar – from a spring in distant hills, for instance – by means of aqueducts. One of the most impressive examples of these aqueducts is the *foggara*, a kind of underground channel

found in Iran and North Africa. A shaft is dug down to a water-bearing layer of rock or aquifer, then a tunnel is excavated to carry the water from the source to the place where it is needed. A distinctive feature of a

foggara is a series of ring-shaped spoil heaps left by its builders in ancient times at the top of the vertical shafts that appear at regular intervals along the line of the tunnel. Some *foggaras* are over 300 ft (91 m) deep and dozens of miles long – a remarkable achievement given that many are of great antiquity. The earliest date back to 2000 BC.

Water dictates the physical appearance of oases. The word oasis is believed to refer to a bowl-like scoop in the desert, derived from an old Egyptian word for a cauldron, and indeed these small pockets of green are often found in picturesque settings, nestling in valleys and hollows, seen perhaps against a backdrop of dramatic mountain ramparts. The limit of cultivated land is marked precisely by the reach of the water, often

DOT TO DOT *Patches of green across the Sahara in Algeria mark the line of a foggara, an underground aqueduct.*

system. As with all life in the desert, these carefully managed microclimates have to adopt, and keep to, rigorous strategies of survival – otherwise, they perish.

SETTLERS V. NOMADS

Oasis dwellers are settled agriculturalists, a system of life which also supports a wide variety of artisans and traders. They had to be self-reliant in the past – they had to make their own bricks out of mud and straw, and roof their houses with palm fronds. All larger oases would have had their own potters, woodcarvers and blacksmiths. But many commodities and luxuries had to be brought in from outside – such as spices, salt, textiles and weapons. Oases served as market places, and many were also staging posts on the great transcontinental trade routes trodden for centuries by caravans of camels.

MASTERS OF THE DESERT
Tuareg men lead a camel caravan across the forbidding Ténéré region of Niger.

resulting in shapes that display a satisfying combination of geometry and nature. In the date-palm groves of North Africa ranks of palms form large, interconnecting rectangles, offset by the graceful curves of the trunks and their heads of fronds. Modern irrigation systems used in Libya and the

4000 wells. This is the most famous of the set of five towns, on the austere M'Zab plateau, which were built at the beginning of the 11th century by the Mozabites, a strict Islamic sect. Even in Ghardaia, however, water is never taken for granted: it has to be used efficiently and with frugality, and distributed fairly. Irrigation systems involve networks of channels and sluicegates, designed to bring water to the fields with the minimum of wastage. Every user bears a responsibility to the system as a whole – and this presupposes a well-orchestrated social

OASIS CITIES

Almost anywhere that is surrounded by desert can qualify as an oasis – and this includes a number of major cities. Damascus, the capital of Syria, has developed on the edge of the Ghouta oasis. It is one of the oldest continuously inhabited cities in the world, with records dating back to 2500 BC. Riyadh, the capital of Saudi Arabia, lies at the very heart of the Arabian Peninsula, a huge tract of land without a single permanent river. The great gambling centre Las Vegas, Nevada, began as an oasis on the route to California; and Tucson in Arizona, surrounded by tracts of desert and mountains, depends for its water on the Ogallala aquifer.

American south-west – in which water is distributed over crops by a long arm rotating on wheels from a central pivot – produce the shock of huge, unearthly discs of green in the midst of flat and arid desert.

Some oasis towns are blessed with copious water. Ghardaia in Algeria is said to have

IMPOSSIBLE WITHOUT THE CAMEL

The camel – the one-humped dromedary – has been an essential part of human life in the deserts of North Africa and the Middle East. Without camels the great desert trading routes and the viability of many oases would have been quite impossible.

Human beings have an extremely limited capacity for travelling and surviving in the desert. Camels, by their unique abilities to survive in arid conditions, can extend the limits of human endurance many times over. It was the Arabs who first called the camel the 'Ship of the Desert': carrying all the supplies needed by their human companions, camels can travel for up to two weeks without eating or drinking. Walking for as long as 18 hours at a stretch, they can cover 20-25 miles (30-40 km) a day – or as much as 125 miles (200 km) in a day if pushed to their limits.

Camels have evolved unique physical features to cope with the conditions of the desert. They have wide two-toed feet that prevent them from sinking into the soft sand. They have long eyelashes to keep sand

THIRSTY WORK *Camels survive for days without drinking, but lap up gallons of water when the opportunity arises.*

out of their eyes, and nostrils that can close in a sandstorm. Their tough mouths and strong teeth allow them to eat thorn bushes and desert scrub. Before a long journey they are made to drink, and they store water in their stomachs. Their humps provide a back-up store of fat which they can draw on when food and water is short.

Camels can lose up to a third of their body weight without coming to harm. They also have a remarkable ability to withstand heat. Their bodies can tolerate a rise in temperature of

9°C (16°F) before they begin to sweat: human beings become ill if their temperature rises 3.3°C (6°F) above normal. Camels lose little water in defecating. However, after a long journey they drink a prodigious quantity of water – as much as 30 gallons (136 litres) at a sitting.

The role of camels is not limited to transport: they provide meat, leather, wool and hair, milk that is made into cheese and yoghurt, and dung that is used as fuel. Racing camels, called hajins, are especially cherished, and can command fabulous prices.

Dromedaries have been domesticated for about 3000 years. There are no truly wild dromedaries left apart from feral ones descended from domesticated herds. There are still some herds of wild Bactrian camels, the two-humped cousin that lives in the desert regions of central and eastern Asia. Bactrian camels serve many of the same functions as dromedaries, and are equally resilient. Their thick, shaggy fur, helps them to survive the bitter winter temperatures of places such as the Gobi Desert.

An underlying theme of many Old World oases is the conflict between settlers and nomads. The nomads are herders. Of necessity, they have fewer material possessions than the settlers and more flexible attitudes towards property and where they belong. However, the divisions between the two are less rigid than they might appear: nomads use the oasis markets to buy and sell, and will often spend a period of the year settled close to one.

Provided that population and resources are in balance, both oasis dwellers and nomadic herders, in their different ways, make the best economic use of the lean resources of the desert. However, the differences in their outlook have often led to strife in the past and still create tension today. Governments – which are usually urban-based – disapprove of the way that nomads roam across national borders and are a law unto themselves. Increasingly, therefore, nomads

are being encouraged – or even forced – to settle. The Tuareg people of the central Sahara, for instance, are facing concerted pressure to give up their nomadic ways. Meanwhile, increasing populations within the oases, the growing aridity of the desert regions, the hardships of desert life and the marginal nature of the desert economy – except where oil and mineral extraction are involved – all threaten to upset the delicate balances on which oases depend.

THE BIG FREEZE

The polar regions present the most consistently hostile

environment in the world: temperatures are well below

zero, there is utter darkness for months at a time, and

most water is locked up in ice. Yet even here there is life.

The temperature is –40°C (–40°F). The entire landscape is in the grip of a deep layer of ice and raked by vicious winds that carry scouring particles of frozen snow. Everything is shrouded in utter blackness – unless the sky is filled with the eerie purple, green or golden glow of the aurora borealis in the north, or the aurora australis in the south, created by incandescent particles from the sun caught in the Earth's magnetic field and colliding with the atmosphere. This is the polar winter, where the sun may not return to bring either warmth or light for weeks or months.

The polar regions are deserts. Despite all the snow, very little of it falls as precipitation, and almost all the fresh water is locked up in ice throughout the year. Oddly, the South Pole has barely measurable precipitation, making it one of the 'driest' places on Earth. The snow is mainly wind-driven particles of ice.

Virtually nothing grows close to the poles. Yet these are extraordinary worlds, where nothing can be taken for granted. Polar bears have been found roaming the ice cap within 12 miles (19 km) of the North Pole. Algae – benefiting from

ICE PALACE *Chinstrap penguins give an idea of scale in the sculptured world of a melting iceberg in Antarctica.*

POLAR TINTS *Lichens and mosses lend colour to the rocks of the Antarctic Peninsula.*

the six months of constant light during the summer – grow in the snow close to the South Pole, feeding off microscopic quantities of dust carried by the wind. These tiny, simple plants, coloured red to protect them from ultra-violet light, produce a bizarre sight in this already unearthly place. Lying just beneath the surface of the snow, they turn large areas of the landscape pink.

The polar regions are so cold because the sun rarely rises far above the horizon. Even in the summer it strikes at an angle, often bathing the landscape in the colours of dawn. The sun's rays have to travel through more of the atmosphere because of this angle, and this absorbs much of their heat. Then the rays are reflected away by the brilliant whiteness of the snow and ice.

Antarctica is colder than the Arctic because it is a landmass, which takes longer to warm up. It is a massive continent, the exact shape and form of which remains a mystery – for most of it is covered by a layer of ice over 1½ miles (2 km) thick. There are mountains, rising to 16 863 ft (5140 m) at the Vinson Massif, and even active volcanoes such as Mount Erebus, as well as the bizarre 'dry valleys' of bare rock and soil which are virtually empty of any snow or ice. More than half of Antarctica is higher

than 10 000 ft (3048 m), making this the continent with the highest average altitude.

Early explorers thought that Antarctica might be just one enormous ice cap until about 1820, when rocks were found around the Antarctic Peninsula, a narrow band of land stretching northwards towards the southern tip of South America. Such rocks are home to the tallest plant of the Antarctic mainland: a lichen that grows to a height of about 2 in (5 cm). The biggest animal that lives permanently on land is a wingless fly, the *Belgica antarctica*, just ³/₁₆ in (4 mm) long. In the company of springtails and mites, it feeds off lichen and mosses, where it also finds some protection against the cold.

It takes great tenacity for any form of life to survive in such conditions, but lichens are exceptional organisms. They are not a true plant or a fungus, but a combination of both – two organisms in one which have lived in an intimate state of symbiosis for 400 million years. The fungi, by secreting tiny quantities of weak acid, are able to extract mineral nutrients from the rocks, but cannot produce chlorophyll to make the starches and sugars that they need. To

SEA AND ICE *Whole fields of snow on South Orkney Island are shaded pink and green by blooms of algae.*

do so they use the captive algae, which in turn feed off the fungi's mineral nutrients. The two elements in lichen reproduce independently, and then the offspring have to find new partners – although small, ready-made scions of an existing partnership may be released or carried away by animals to form new colonies elsewhere. They paint the rocks in a dazzling array of textured patterns, from ochre polka dots to black whorls. Because of the very short growing season, they may increase in size only fractionally each year – and so the larger colonies represent hundreds, even thousands, of years of growth.

Recent discoveries of fossil leaves on Seymour Island, off the Antarctic Peninsula, show that this continent was not always a snowy wasteland. Up to about 40 million years ago there were forests of beech trees and ferns here, inhabited by marsupials. At that time the Earth was warmer and there

FISHY ANTIFREEZE *The body of the Antarctic cod* (Notothenia angustifrons) *is protected by a form of antifreeze.*

FENDING OFF THE COLD
A thick layer of blubber insulates an elephant seal from the intense cold.

were no ice caps. Antarctica was also probably farther north then. It had been a part of the giant ancient continent called Gondwanaland, which split up some 150 million years ago. Antarctica slowly moved southwards and took up its present position about 6.5 million years ago. The Earth has since passed through a series of climate fluctuations from warm to cold. Five million years ago the polar ice caps were half as big again as they are today.

ANTIFREEZE AND BLUBBER

There may be little permanent life on land in Antarctica, but there is plenty in the seas around it. Not only are the seas warmer than the land; they also contain huge quantities of phytoplankton and the minute crustaceans known as krill which feed on it – both of which are at the important lower end of a huge food chain of carnivores. Just about every animal in these waters is potential food for something else, and only the largest, such as the blue whales, have no fear of predators – apart from man. The aggression in this food chain is no better illustrated than by the violence with which a leopard seal will take a swimming penguin,

or the way that a killer whale will suddenly launch itself onto a beach to snatch an unsuspecting sea lion.

The animals that live in and around such waters must have some means of coping with the intense cold. Some species of fish, such as the notothenioids, have been found to contain a kind of antifreeze called glycoprotein, which prevents their blood from turning to ice. Penguins, and mammals such as seals and whales, are protected from the cold by layers of blubber. This is so effective that the internal temperature of a seal may be 42°C (76°F) warmer than its skin temperature. Bodies tend to be bulky and limbs small, both for streamlining in water and to conserve heat. Male elephant seals, the largest of the seal family, reach lengths of 20ft (6m) and weigh up to 4 tons.

Despite this insulation, few Antarctic animals choose to remain on the continent through the dark winter. They come to their breeding grounds on the edge of the ice during the spring, where they multiply in astronomic numbers, supported by the immense wealth of food in the sea. But as winter draws in, they head north once more to the marginally gentler climate of the peripheral islands.

A typical example is the elephant seal. It is not its size that has given this seal its name so much as the male's trunk-like snout. The male inflates this during the breeding season

to make his roar more impressive. During this period, elephant seals congregate in large numbers on various islands bordering the Antarctic, such as South Georgia, the Kerguelen Islands, the South Shetlands and on the coast of southern Argentina. The south Georgia colony numbers as many as 300 000 seals.

Males fight for control of their females, and when at his fittest, about ten years old, a male will command a harem of up to 40 females. Mating occurs in September, and pups are born about six weeks later. A month after this, the pups are weaned and ready to take to the sea, but by this time the mother is pregnant again, producing a second pup in early December. The seals then head for the open sea to feed, returning to the breeding grounds for the annual moult towards the end of the summer, when the winter coat is prepared by shedding the hair and skin of the old one. During the moulting season, the colony nuzzles up together for warmth in dense heaps, beneath a cloud of flaking skin and hair, and the tensions that are so apparent during the breeding season are set aside.

SEAS OF ICE

Over the winter the ice covering the sea around the continent of Antarctica will have increased sevenfold. Salt water freezes at a temperature of –1.9°C (35.4°F), and as

THE INUIT — LIFE IN THE COLD

In April 1909 the American Robert Peary claimed to have reached the North Pole – the first person to do so. Two and a half years later the Norwegian Roald Amundsen became the first person to reach the South Pole. They were two of the most determined polar explorers of their day, who achieved their goals after many years of experience in the Arctic. They had two things in common: their zeal and their respect for the Inuit (Eskimos). They owed their success to the Inuit skills they adopted – their dog sleds, their fur clothes, even their food.

Inuit life is brilliantly adapted to the harsh conditions of the Arctic. The first people to inhabit the northern shores of Asia and North America were probably part of a steady movement of people across the Bering Strait – then a land bridge – at the end of the last Ice Age, about 10000 years ago. These ice-bound northern lands were bitterly cold, but they offered good hunting. The Inuit have lived by hunting ever since, or at least until this century.

In the past, animals provided for most of their needs. They kept warm by dressing in furs: their winter clothes consisted of two, remarkably lightweight layers of high boots, trousers and hooded tunics. Bones were used to make harpoons, tools and needles, and even sleds. Their boats were made of animal skins. Their homes were lit by lamps that burnt blubber. In winter they used huskies to draw their sleds. This extremely tough breed of dog, originally from Siberia, can live outdoors in almost all weathers.

The Inuit tended to spend winter in their villages – clusters of houses made of rocks and turf, with beams of driftwood or whalebone. Sometimes igloos were used as winter quarters. With no windows and low doorways to keep out the cold, and occupied by several families, these homes would remain snug, if somewhat fuggy.

In summer the Inuit communities would disperse in search of game – hunting for seals, walruses, fish, birds, or gathering berries and roots. What they did not eat, they dried and stored for the winter.

It was a life of immense hardship, and naturally vulnerable to the lure of an easier life that Western-style civilisation offered. Now many Inuit live in prefabricated houses, equipped with central heating, refrigerators and telephones. But there are few

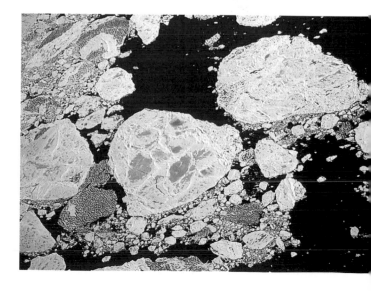

DRESSED TO KILL *The fur clothing of the Inuit (above) is light and supple. The crush of freezing ice floes (left) creates a platform from which a hunter can scan the horizon.*

Western-style jobs at these high latitudes to go with this imported lifestyle, and as traditional skills are lost, there is little to replace the occupations that made sense of the harsh environment. However, a recent effort by Inuit groups to revive and preserve the distinctive aspects of their culture and values may yet prevent the traditions of their way of life from being lost for ever.

it does so it first of all becomes strangely soupy. Then it forms vast expanses of flat, broken polygons called 'pancake ice', sometimes decorated with delicate ice flowers created as the freezing seawater forms around crystals of salt. Finally these ice floes bind together as pack ice in a tight but unstable bond. The vast force of expanding ice causes loud groans and cracks, and in the past turned many of the wooden-hulled ships of the early explorers and mariners into kindling wood.

In late spring the reverse process occurs, and during the melt huge hunks of ice, some the size of European countries, may come away from the thick ice shelves that line the deep bays of the continent. These float off as flat-topped icebergs, their great depth signalled only by the gradations of turquoise and blue that frame the upper contours of their submarine bulk.

The Arctic is the inverse of Antarctica, and not simply because it is at the other end of the globe. Antarctica is an island

FLAT PACK *The pack ice around the north coast of Greenland is a maze of ice floes that break up over the summer.*

CHILLING OUT *In warmer weather, a polar bear sometimes has to cool off by lying on its back in the snow.*

surrounded by ocean; the Arctic is an ocean virtually surrounded by land. The North Pole passes through not a continent of land but an ice cap which floats on top of the Arctic Ocean. Submarines have passed over the North Pole. This, then, is a world which consists entirely of ice – ice that not only

---

COOLING OFF

Under their thick, white fur polar bears have black skin, which absorbs heat, and a layer of subcutaneous blubber, which insulates them so effectively that they can swim for hours in water that would kill a human being in minutes. This protection against the cold does, however, have disadvantages. Polar bears cannot run long distances when pursuing prey without becoming very hot; they tend, therefore, to make quick and sudden dashes. In summer they may become uncomfortably warm. In such circumstances they lie on their backs on snow banks, limbs akimbo, and allow their body heat to disperse from the shorter belly hairs.

---

expands and contracts, but is constantly on the move under the force of great ocean currents. Carried by the same currents, and sometimes floating far to the south of the region, are the icebergs that have 'calved' off glaciers. Sculpted by the wind and water

into unearthly shapes – huge spires, dunce's hats, mathematical hedrons, animal shapes and arches – they drift silently through the open seas like ghostly carnival floats.

Again, this polar region is the domain of carnivores. Seals, sea birds and marine mammals feed on the vast shoals of fish and crustaceans. Animal populations can reach huge numbers. Walruses, for instance, pack the shores of islands close to the Bering Strait, forming slumbering piles of pinky-brown flesh spiked with their long, curving tusks.

But the king of the ice is undoubtedly the polar bear. Polar bears are usually solitary creatures that roam the ice floes looking for their favourite food, seals. Directed to their prey by their acute sense of smell, they are able to kill it with a mighty swat of their powerful forelimbs. In winter they move

PURPLE HIGHLIGHTS *Purple saxifrage produces a rare burst of colour during the long days of the Arctic summer.*

southwards where they gather in groups and then settle in dens carved out of the snow and ice. Cubs are born, almost hairless, in midwinter, but are kept warm by their mother and nourished by her fat-rich milk.

THE OUTER RIM

In winter the sea ice of the Arctic Ocean thickens, locking tightly on to the rim of land formed by Canada, Greenland, Scandinavia and Russia. But during the brief Arctic summer the snow and ice melts on most of this land, and it is rapidly transformed into a more habitable world. A surprising number of plants then spring into life. These include not only the tough grasses and woody, ground-clinging shrubs and trees, such as heaths, willow and juniper, but also lupins, delicate primroses, Arctic poppies, and alpines such as mountain avens and mountain forget-me-nots. They survive the cold through a variety of adaptations. Some of the more vulnerable plants, for instance, are covered in fine hairs, which provide insulation. Others, such as moss campion and saxifrage, grow in tightly bunched cushions, which keep in any precious warmth.

These plants and the warmer weather attract animals that have spent the winter in the tundra farther south, such as caribou, while birds such as snow geese, dovekies, red-throated loons, thick-billed murres fly in from their wintering grounds all over the world. Mallards winter in California, golden

plovers in Argentina, wheatears in Africa, but the world's greatest traveller is the Arctic tern, which spends the Southern Hemisphere's summer in the Antarctic and the Northern Hemisphere's summer in the Arctic, an annual journey of some 25000 miles (40000 km).

Some animals, however, such as Arctic wolves, hares, ground squirrels and lemmings stay throughout the year in these frozen wastes. To keep warm mammals can shiver to stimulate their metabolism, but this expends energy which uses up valuable reserves of fat or demands fresh intakes of food. The alternative is to lower the metabolism and hibernate, a strategy used by some of the smaller mammals which live in burrows. Protected by a layer of snow in winter, the temperature in the burrow may hover at around freezing point, many degrees warmer than the temperature outside. Various birds also make a permanent home in and around the Arctic, such as the snowy owl, rock ptarmigan, Arctic polls and snow buntings. To keep warm, birds will fluff up their feathers and bury themselves in a blanket of snow.

Ellesmere Island, the northernmost part of Canada, presents a good view of the possibilities of life within the Arctic Circle. It is a large island, its tip reaching to within 470 miles (756 km) of the North Pole. Indeed, it was here that many expeditions made their base camp for their attempts to reach the North Pole, including the one led by the American Robert Peary in 1909. Although winter temperatures drop to −45°C (−49°F), in the summer between late June and late August temperatures average 7°C (45°F), and in pockets may reach 21°C (70°F). With just 2½in (60 mm) of rainfall a year, the island is essentially a desert, but nonetheless in the summer the valleys are

THE MIDNIGHT SUN

The closer you are to the Poles, the longer the summer days. This is because of the 23.5° tilt of the Earth as it circles the sun. During summer months in the Northern Hemisphere, the top of the Earth tilts towards the sun. At a latitude of, say, 60° North, which cuts through the Shetland Isles and Oslo, the sun barely dips beneath the horizon during the brief midsummer nights. Farther north,

at 66°32' North, lies the Arctic Circle. This imaginary line marks the most southerly point at which the sun does not set at all in summer: On the Arctic Circle it does this just once, on Midsummer's Day, around June 21. The sun dips low in the sky, but never drops beneath the horizon. Farther north still, as the Earth curves towards the Pole, the period during which the midnight sun can be seen is extended

from several days to weeks and months. At the North Pole itself, the sun does not set for six months, from March 21 to September 23 – the equinoxes. At the winter equinox at the North Pole the sun circles the horizon, then it drops below it. The daylight fades into thickening shades of grey before the long, dark winter sets in – and the inverse process begins in the Southern Hemisphere.

ANGLES OF ATTACK *The tilt of the Earth as it orbits the sun dictates the angle at which the sun's rays strike the Earth through the year.*

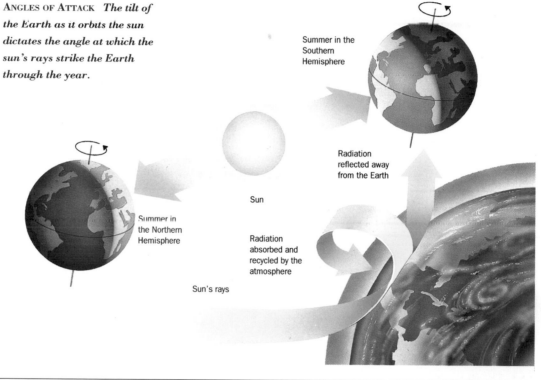

Summer in the Southern Hemisphere

Summer in the Northern Hemisphere

Sun

Radiation reflected away from the Earth

Radiation absorbed and recycled by the atmosphere

Sun's rays

ablaze with poppies and lupins which feed on the meltwater. Being an island, winter migration southwards across the tundra is not feasible. The land animals that live here stay for the whole year. They include herds of Peary's caribou, smaller and paler than their better-known relatives farther south, and musk oxen. It is a land as remote and majestic as any in the world, with mountains scored by huge, creaking glaciers and vast, bare valleys dappled with lakes that glint in the chill, crystal-clear air.

STURDY SURVIVORS *Musk oxen often stand in closely packed herds to protect themselves against predators and the cold.*

NEXT TO THE HEAVENS

Only a few thousand yards may stand between rain forests and snowy mountain peaks, environments as different as the tropics and poles. In between may be islands of life isolated from the outside world, places unlike anywhere else on Earth.

Mountain peaks, capped by snow and brushed by racing clouds, cast a spell of their own. Their aloof, breathtaking beauty and changing moods have long inspired comparisons with human characteristics, and have been woven into countless legends and myths. Mount Everest is known by the Tibetans as *Chomolungma,* 'Goddess Mother of the World'. Mount Kailas in south-western Tibet – a near perfect pyramid close to the sources of the Brahmaputra, the Indus, the Sutlej and the Karnali, a tributary of the Ganges – is sacred to Hindus and Buddhists alike, and the focus of gruelling pilgrimages. Even without religious associations, many peaks around the world inspire awe and wonderment, such as the extraordinary pink granite pinnacles of the Paine Horns in southern Chile.

It is said of mountains in the world's more temperate regions that climbing 1000 ft (300 m) represents a change of environment equivalent to 300 miles (500 km) of latitude towards the poles. Most mountains, therefore, are banded by ecological rings which provide a gradual succession of habitats from the foothills to the peak. The eastern Himalayas, for instance, rise from subtropical forest through deciduous ones, with bamboo and grass, to temperate forests containing chestnuts and

SHINING SPIRES *The granite of the Torres del Paine in Chile glows in the dawn light.*

MOUNTAIN GOATS — SURE-FOOTED ATHLETES

If there is any animal built for a life on the steep slopes of mountains it is the American mountain goat. In fact, it seems to seek out the steepest escarpments, springing over precipitous rocks in a way that appears to defy both gravity and good sense. No other animal can compete in this terrain, and mountain goats will sometimes be seen grazing in close proximity to predators such as bears, confident in the knowledge that their enemies will not dare to pursue them.

Despite the common name, the mountain goat (*Oreamnos americanus*) is not a true goat, but a goat-antelope, like its distant relative the chamois. It lives in the western mountains of North America, on the edge of the timberline at altitudes over 10 000 ft (3050 m) – in the northern Rockies and parallel coastal mountains from Alaska to Idaho. Its sturdy, rectangular body and head are supported by short, muscular legs, with flexible, two-toed hooves that give it extra grip on the rocks. To fend off the cold of winters which may last eight months, mountain goats have thick greasy underwool, with an upper layer of 8 in (20 cm) guard hairs; they shed their coats in spring.

There is little outward difference between males and females: both billies and nannies have beards and horns, and both can become very belligerent, especially at mating time in October and November. The young are born in spring, and begin climbing and gambolling within 48 hours of birth. Mountain goats tend to congregate in small herds, dappling steep rock faces where they browse on grasses, lichen and wild flowers.

KING OF THE CASTLE *The American mountain goat is one of the most sure-footed of all mountain animals.*

oaks, maple and alder. At about 8800 ft (2700 m) conifer forests take over, interspersed with rhododendron and juniper. By 11 800 ft (3600 m) these have thinned out and given way to alpine meadows of resilient grasses and the kind of summer-flowering plants found in the tundra. Above this lie the icy peaks where, with the exception of the thin air, conditions are similar to those of the polar regions.

Closer to the Equator the gradations are intensified. Even on the Equator itself, mountains such as Mount Kenya – 17 060 ft (5200 m) above sea level – rise to peaks majestically capped with snow.

Local conditions bring further variety to this scheme. Mountain worlds are riddled with microclimates, where orientation towards the sun and shelter from the wind make a difference that may be the equivalent of hundreds of feet in altitude. The resulting conditions may be unique.

Close to a high pass on the border between Chile and Argentina sharp pinnacles of frozen snow, 6-20 ft (1.8-6 m) high, march down the slope in a bizarre procession that reminded people of Catholic penitents in their conical hoods, and so were named Los Penitentes. No one knows quite why they take on this shape, but one theory is that the dry air creates electrical fields which have an effect on the continual process of freezing and melting as the surrounding temperature varies.

HIGHLAND LIFE

The highland regions of Tibet, by contrast, provide an ecosystem on a huge scale, with vast empty spaces of rocky peaks, scree slopes and broad valleys washed by torrential rivers after the spring melt. The air is so thin and clear at these heights that distances become hard to judge. From high passes, ranks of mountain ridges can be seen fading away in the dry, cloudless air towards the far horizon, etched by a succession of delicate hues – ochre, pink, mauve and blue. Such landscapes formed the backdrop for many remote Tibetan Buddhist monasteries, often set high above valleys where villagers farm pockets of emerald-green fields next to river courses. Much of this religious tradition has been erased by the Chinese in Tibet itself, but survives in Ladakh, a neighbouring province belonging to India.

There are huge areas of Tibet which – because they are so inhospitable and remote – have never seen a settled human population. The Chang Tang region that stretches across the north of Tibet is an arid grassland set 16 000 ft (4875 m) above sea level. This wilderness is home to select specialists, such as Tibetan woolly hares, black-lipped pikas, lynxes, Tibetan brown bears, grazing herds of Tibetan antelopes (in fact, a relative

MOUNTAIN LEGACY *Dozens of Buddhist monasteries now lie in ruins across Tibet.*

HIGH LIFE · *Neither Himalayan yaks (left) nor Andean alpacas (above) can live comfortably below 13 000 ft (400 m).*

of sheep and goats), wild asses, argali sheep and wild yaks.

The yak is designed for the mountains – and indeed finds it hard to survive at heights lower than 13 750 ft (4200 m). It has an immensely heavy coat, which it sheds each

ABOVE THE SNOW LINE

The snow line marks the limit of permanent snow on a mountain. On the Equator it comes at about 16 500 ft (5000 m), in Europe at 9000 ft (2750 m). Temperatures above the snow line often drop to –20°C (–4°F). Few animals live permanently above it, except for some small insects such as springtails and grylloblattids, whose bodies seem to be immune to the cold. Birds, however, often venture to these heights. Condors soar above the Andes at heights of up to 23 000 ft (7000 m); choughs have been seen close to the top of Mount Everest.

summer. Yaks are used as a beast of burden in the Himalayas, but they also pull ploughs and provide a rich milk which is commonly made into the fermented butter that is mixed with tea to produce the common broth-like hot drink of the Himalayas.

The yak's adaptation to high altitudes is mirrored in the Andes by the llama. This

distant relative of the camel family has been domesticated for 4000 years, and, like the yak, is more than just a beast of burden. Its dense wool wards off the cold, though it is considered less fine than the long fleece of its cousin, the alpaca. There are also two wild relatives, the guanaco and the vicuña, the most graceful of the llama family.

ROOF GARDENS

The higher the altitude, the more stringent the conditions for plant life. As in the tundra, plants cope in different ways with the problems of the cold, rarefied environment and the short growing seasons of mountain tops. Many are perennials and reproduce from rhizomes and bulbs, and usually have extensive root networks to survive the high winds. Some plants, such as edelweiss, have woolly textures to protect them from the cold. A Himalayan daisy called the saussurea produces a flower like a shapeless woolly hat, covered in white filaments.

Cold-weather plants generally produce new buds in spring, but because of the short growing season near the snow line, the alpine snowbell produces buds at the end of the previous winter. These leap into

WARMLY FELT · *The felt-like texture of the edelweiss flower is a form of natural insulation.*

action as soon as the spring melt begins, producing the surprising spectacle of delicate flowers growing from a field of snow.

High in the mountains of Tasmania giant cushion plants have developed over hundreds of years. Containing up to six species of plant, they grow as tightly bunched communities to protect themselves from the cold and preserve warmth and moisture. Gradually, debris from previous years' growth builds up, forming large and remarkably firm hillocks several feet across.

By contrast, the puya plants of the Andes grow in splendid isolation. Relatives of the pineapple, their almost spherical rosettes, 4 ft (1.2 m) across, dot the barren landscape where little other growth begins to compete – for example, around the immense Colca Canyon in Peru. After many decades, a huge spike rises 13-20 ft (4-4 m) from the sphere and bursts into a display of thousand of flowers.

The trees growing on Yellow Mountain – in fact a cluster of 72 peaks in southern Anhui province, China – are also spectacular in their isolation. High on the tips of pinnacles of rock that rise to 5900 ft (1800 m), pine trees somehow manage to find a toehold and gradually grow to full size. Striking statuesque silhouettes and often set above a sea of clouds, the peaks have been a famous inspiration to Chinese poets and painters for centuries.

Like sea around an island, altitude can create a kind of hermetic isolation. In New Zealand, Mount Egmont (also known as Mount Taranaki) is an almost

FLOWER PILLARS *After decades without flowering, a puya plant will produce a huge spike bearing thousands of flowers.*

EAST AFRICA'S GIANT LOBELIAS

In Europe lobelia are best known as dainty, flowering plants that trail in blue and purple clumps from window boxes. In the mountains of East Africa they take on another dimension. Here giant lobelias form huge rosettes of lance-shaped leaves. One species secretes a kind of slime which, mixed with rainwater, accumulates in the rosette. It prevents the water from evaporating in the heat of the day; by night a thin layer of ice protects the buds in the base of the rosette from cold. When this species flowers, it produces a flower spike, draped with silvery, hair-like bracts. Again, these act as insulation. The flowers themselves lie close to the stalk, protected by the hairs. This makes them accessible only to the plant's preferred pollinators, such as the long-beaked malachite sunbird, attracted by sweet-smelling nectar.

CARNIVAL OF MONSTERS
A rocket-shaped giant lobelia thrusts upwards among woolly looking giant groundsels.

perfect volcanic cone, rising rapidly to 8261 ft (2518 m) from the pasturelands in the south-western corner of the North Island. Native trees such as the rimu and the rata, which grows around a host tree like a strangler fig, cloak the lower slopes up to about 3000 ft (900 m), while kaikawaka and totara trees grow higher up before the woodlands give way to alpine meadows. Once these trees grew widely across the whole area, but have been cleared for farming. Now the slopes of Mount Egmont provide them with a sanctuary.

GIANT CABBAGES

Perhaps the most unusual of all isolated mountain environments is found in East Africa. Mount Kenya, the Ruwenzori Mountains and the volcanic mountains of the

Virunga Range all rise to over 14 750 ft (4500 m). Here, beneath the snowline lies a remarkable world of tussock meadows and outsized plants – giant lobelia with their towering headdresses and giant groundsels that grow like palm trees, 40 ft (12 m) tall, with their trunks swathed in a duvet of dead leaves. On the higher slopes are monstrous kitchen gardens filled with so-called cabbage groundsels.

By night temperatures at this high altitude drop to below freezing, and water in the ponds and in the rosettes of some lobelias freezes over. By day the equatorial sun pours down through clear skies. No one is quite sure why these plants have opted for gigantism in their evolution, but it may well be to cope with these extremes of temperature. Other features besides size bolster their defences, such as silvery leaves to reflect the sun, and velvety textures and hairs to create layers of insulation against the extremes of both cold and heat. Cabbage groundsels also arch their leaves over their buds to fend off the cold at night.

SELF-QUILTING *In the chill air of Mount Kenya, giant groundsels retain the blackened remnants of dead foliage to insulate their trunks.*

SHOW OF STRENGTH *On the forested slopes of the Virunga Mountains, a male mountain gorilla displays his power.*

Among the few animals living at this altitude is a long-haired hyrax, which feeds off the leaves of the giant lobelia. Although it looks like a cross between a cat and a fox, it is in fact a relative of the elephant. The branches of the family split about 65 million years ago, and the similarities are seen only in the ear and leg bones.

At about 10 000 ft (3000 m) on the Virunga mountains are giant heathers, and trees draped with orchids and mosses, from which this ecological layer has been dubbed the 'Place of Beards'. Lower down, the landscape drops through a range of more conventional habitats, from bamboo forests to tropical rain forests inhabited by chameleons, palm-nut vultures, civets and monkeys. The tropical forests of the Virunga mountains also provide a refuge for another species that is not found elsewhere: the mountain gorillas. These vegetarian giants live in groups of up to 30 animals. They forage by day and at night build themselves nests from branches and foliage. Forest clearance had reduced their domain to just 285 sq miles (738 km²).

REBORN FROM THE ASHES

Volcanic eruptions and fires create scarred landscapes of cinders and ash, shattered trees and contorted lava. Slowly – or sometimes remarkably swiftly – nature recolonises the devastated area, first with plants, and then with animals.

When Krakatoa erupted in August 1883 an island was blown right out of the sea. It was the most destructive eruption of recent times: some 36 000 people were killed as a tidal wave tore through the villages on the neighbouring coasts of Sumatra and Java. The boom was heard 2200 miles (3500 km) away in Australia. Ten days later dust from the volcano fell 3313 miles (5330 km) away, and weather patterns across the world were affected for years because of airborne debris.

Nine months after the blast scientists landed on the island of Rakata, the only surviving part of the ancient caldera from which Krakatoa had emerged. They found just one spider among the deep layers of sterile ash and pumice. But over the following months the ash was dispersed by the region's heavy rainfall – some 100 in (2540 mm) per annum – to reveal the fertile soil of the old volcano. Two years later there were 28 plant species, including algae, mosses and ferns, grasses and conifers. Now there are about 200, forming dense woodland. All arrived from neighbouring landmasses, by sea, on the air and brought by birds. A wide variety of animals have also made the journey, including spiders, beetles, ants, land crabs, geckos, monitor lizards, reticulated pythons, rats and fruit bats.

Then in 1927 a new, active volcanic cone began to grow up from the seabed where Krakatoa had stood 44 years earlier. Named Anak Krakatoa, Child of Krakatoa, it presented a unique opportunity to see how nature colonises a virgin landscape. This island posed different problems to those of Rakata. Here the land consists of fresh black lava, and the volcano remains highly active, occasionally spewing forth debris and sulphurous vapour. Even so, at the more sheltered eastern end of the island, grasses, ferns, wild sugar and convolvulus began to take hold, followed by pandanus pines and casuarina trees, which provided a habitat for bats. Meanwhile, beneath the surface of the sea coral reefs began to re-establish

CAUGHT STANDING *Lava from Nyiragongo in the Virunga Mountains of central Africa encases the lower trunks of trees demolished in its path.*

HAWAIIAN BEAUTY
Silverswords grow from
the unpromising soil of
Hawaiian lava flows.

themselves, and they were soon inhabited by as rich a variety of sea life as before 1883.

Volcanoes offer a uniquely tough environment for plants and animals to survive in. Although volcanic soil eventually becomes highly fertile, it is initially brittle, poorly drained and starved of nitrogen. Black basalt, which absorbs the heat of the sun, is particularly unfavourable. A few plants, however, seem to thrive in this harsh environment, finding adequate soil, moisture and nutrients for growth, and building up pockets of richer soil through their decay and the debris left behind by visiting animals. This process of rehabilitation is often led by lichen, blue-green algae, mosses and ferns.

Some volcanic landscapes are dominated by one plant. Cacti, for instance, grow in the unpromising volcanic terrain of the Galápagos Islands. Violets grow on the scree slopes of Mount Etna in Sicily, Europe's largest active volcano. The most remarkable volcano plant is the Hawaiian silversword.

MOST VIOLENT VOLCANO

It has been estimated that Krakatoa erupted with a force hundreds of times stronger than that of the atomic bomb on Hiroshima. It was not, however, the greatest explosion known. In 1815, Mount Tambora on the Indonesian island of Sumbawa erupted, discharging eight times the amount of debris that Krakatoa did. Perhaps the largest explosion in history was when the Mediterranean island of Santorini erupted in about 1500 BC. This catastrophic explosion may have been responsible for the destruction of the Minoan civilisation.

There are three species of silversword on the islands of Maui and Hawaii at altitudes of 9000-14 000 ft (2750-4250 m). The most spectacular, *Argyroxiphum sandwicensis spp.*

macrocephalum, has a mass of pointed, silvery leaves forming a neat sphere. It grows on the cinder slopes of Mount Haleakala on Maui. The silver helps to deflect the heat of the sun. After 15 to 50 years the plant will thrust up a huge 6½-10 ft (2-3 m) tall flower spike bearing some 600 flowers resembling deep-red daisies. Then the plant dies. Silverswords are, in fact, members of the daisy family, and their closest equivalents appear to be the tarweeds that grow in California and Chile. The first silversword must have arrived either with a bird, or on the sea, since the Hawaiian islands were never a part of another continent, but rose from the seabed as volcanoes.

Another Hawaiian plant specially adapted to the volcanic landscape is the ohia lehua tree, known for its scarlet flowers. Hawaiian volcanoes tend to erupt comparatively gently, but repeatedly, sending rivers of molten lava and hot cinders down their flanks. Provided that its bark is not scorched all around its trunk, the ohia lehua can tolerate avalanches of hot cinders. Surviving

MOUNT ST HELENS: WATCHING NATURE RETURN

On May 18, 1980, the north-western states of the USA witnessed one of the most dramatic volcanic eruptions of this century. Mount St Helens stood at the centre of a parkland cherished by hikers and nature lovers. After months of rumblings, the entire cap of the volcano was blasted northwards, reducing the height of the mountain by 1300 ft (396 m) in a matter of seconds.

The volcano contained deposits of silica-rich sedimentary rock which does not create the kind of flows of soft molten lava seen, for instance, on Hawaii. Instead it forms a type of thick, compact magma which packs hard over the cone as pressure builds up relentlessly beneath it. In the case of Mount St Helens, this culminated in the catastrophic explosion, which sent a plume of dust like an atomic mushroom cloud 60 000 ft (18 300 m) high into the sky and blasted millions of tons of debris into the valley below.

Despite two months of warnings, 57 people were killed by the eruption as 230 sq miles (595 km²) of forest and lakes were overwhelmed by superheated gases and a tidal wave

of rocks, rubble and ash. Spirit Lake, a famous beauty spot to the north of the mountain, was utterly transformed as it was thrust upwards dozens of feet on a raft of debris. A series of smaller eruptions convulsed the volcano for nearly two years.

At first the reaction was one of horror at the extent of the destruction. But it was soon decided that a virtue should be made of necessity: the park was designated a recovery zone – carefully protected and monitored, but essentially left to its own devices to see how nature recolonises such a scene of devastation.

One surprise was the number of animals which had survived the extreme conditions during the eruption. Despite surface temperatures estimated at 300°C (570°F), pocket gophers were protected by their burrows, while some fish found shelter in the depths of the lakes. Within a year the most tenacious colonisers of the plant world had started to take root in the dusty, nitrogen-starved soil. These included fireweed, or willowherb, the purple-flowered plant that was commonly found in London bomb-sites during the Second World War. Others, such as avalanche lilies, monkey flowers, lupin and bracken

fern followed, and later again came Douglas fir and Pacific silver fir. In the vanguard of recolonising animals were spiders, moths, flies and dragonflies, which came to feed on the plant debris; then came ground squirrels, chipmunks and even beavers. Ducks and ospreys flew in to feed on the burgeoning water life in the nutrient-rich lakes; and soon even herds of Roosevelt elk returned to browse on the young plants.

More than 15 years later, however, Mount St Helens bears the raw scars of its savage wounds. The 'blast zone' under the volcano is blanketed with deep layers of debris and looks like a desert. But at the same time, this area, with its softened contours of gentle pastel colours extending across the vast expanse of barren debris, is also a place of haunting and majestic beauty.

BLAST ZONE *The eruption of Mount St Helens pulverised the entire summit of the mountain and cast tons of debris into a fan-shaped area to the north. Forests up to 17 miles (27 km) away were flattened.*

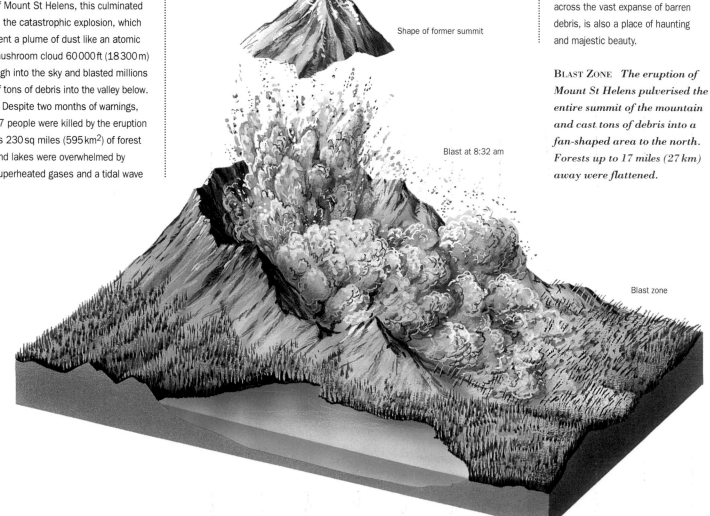

Shape of former summit

Blast at 8:32 am

Blast zone

ribbons of bark are enough to support the leaves, and after the damage is done the tree puts on a rapid spurt of growth.

CLEANSING FIRES

Volcanoes smother landscapes with debris. Fires, by comparison, bring more temporary destruction. They can move through a landscape with devastating swiftness, leaving behind the charred and smouldering remains of all that stood in their path. In a forest this might include arboreal animals that cannot move out of the way quickly enough. Ash, however, is nutritious, and after rains new life will soon return to the land, although it may take many years to rebuild the ecosystem.

Because they recover more quickly, fire-affected landscapes offer a valuable opportunity to observe succession – the successive ecosystems that take over a landscape, replacing one another until equilibrium is reached. This equilibrium, the ecosystem best suited to the environment, is called the climax community. After a woodland fire, for instance, grasses may be first to grow, but these will later be overshadowed by shrubs. Then the trees will begin to reassert their dominance and restore the wood to its original form, and eventually the climax community will be re-established. Each stage in the process attracts its own set of animals.

It is not always as simple as that, however. Where fires are a frequent hazard – under active volcanoes, for instance, or on grasslands that are regularly struck by lightning – ecosystems may develop in which the dominant plants actually need fire to assert themselves, and are programmed by evolution to recover quickly.

In Australia a number of plants survive fire, such as the grass trees. These grow as exuberant heads of sword-like leaves on top of compact and fibrous trunks formed by

BACK TO NORMAL *Just eight weeks after devastating bush fires in 1994, eucalyptus trees near Sydney began to recover.*

the hard bases of previous years' growths of leaves. When fire passes, the leaves burn off, but the trunk remains more or less impervious, and will sprout new leaves three months later. Other Australian plants, such as the various eucalyptus trees, have bark that catches fire, but only the outer bark is damaged, leaving the tree alive, if scorched. Some of the spectacular Banksia family of flowering plants, such as *Banksia incana*, have seeds that split apart only after fire.

The old prairie grasslands of central USA depend on fire to preserve them in

CUT-LEAF BEAUTY
The cut-leaf Banksia, like many of its family, shows a remarkable resilience to fire.

FLAME FLOWERS

One of the most spectacular groups of flowering shrubs and trees, the Proteas, grows in the *fynbos*, dry scrubland in the south-east of South Africa. The flowers vary considerably, but the most striking look like sunbursts, and have the geometric complexity, robust texture and hairy qualities of an artichoke.

Every 5 to 40 years, fire sweeps through the dry *fynbos* – yet this is the habitat in which proteas thrive. The seeds actually need the heat of the fire to burn off the seed-coat and

start germinating. Proteas are much sought-after by horticulturalists, but the propagation of some species has remained elusive. We now know that

some proteas need not just heat to germinate, but also the chemical content of smoke, notably ethylene and ammonia, to trigger the process.

KING OF THE FYNBOS *The king protea produces silky-haired flowers the size of a soup bowl.*

caused by volcanoes or glaciers. In recent times, it has been the scale and speed of human destruction that has left nature gasping for breath, and in many places the destruction of ecosystems has been so complete that extinction has resulted, making recovery impossible.

Nature, however, shows great resilience. Between 1946 and 1958 the United States carried out 23 atomic tests on the Pacific atoll of Bikini, including the detonation of a hydrogen bomb 1000 times more powerful than the one dropped on Hiroshima. The coral reef was pulverised, and the land rendered so radioactive that the island's former inhabitants are still not allowed to return. Scientists expected that the ocean floor would be a desert for many decades, but already the seas around the atoll are swarming with life – with crabs, corals, and shoals of snapper, jacks and yellow-finned goat fish. It seems that the forces of life will reassert themselves, even against the longest odds.

their natural state. The grass, which sprouts from underground roots, is able to survive the fire, while the shrubs that compete with it are burnt off. Without the fires the shrubs would begin to dominate and eventually the landscape would turn to forest.

The aromatic shrubs of the dry maquis country of southern France – such as rosemary, thyme and sage – contain volatile oils that make them cherished as culinary herbs. These oils are highly flammable and they burn quickly in a fire. After a fire, however, they come into their own. Grasses are the first to recover, but then the aromatic shrubs start to spring back. Their oils serve two purposes: they discourage the growth of any competitors, and are distasteful to browsing animals. So, as the shrubs recover, the grasses die back, poisoned by the shrubs' roots and cropped by animals. The aromatic shrubs, however, need fire to prevent domination by the next

level of succession – trees. Their volatile oils, in assisting the fires, help them to maintain their dominance.

HUMAN DESTRUCTION

By and large, the destruction of habitats by humans is no different from that wrought by other causes and, until the last 200 years, was less significant than the destruction

HEALING THE WOUNDS
Snappers were among the first creatures to recolonise the reefs of Bikini atoll after 12 years of atomic tests.

LOST IN SPACE 4

WET AND WILD *Land and water mix in the inland tundra landscape of Iceland.*

THE STEPPES OF SOUTHERN RUSSIA, THE GRASSLANDS OF EAST AFRICA, THE TUNDRA OF SIBERIA AND CANADA — ALL ARE EFFECTIVELY MICROCLIMATES WRIT LARGE, WHERE SPECIAL WEATHER PATTERNS AND TERRAIN HAVE CREATED MASSIVE, OPEN HABITATS, WITH SIMILAR TYPES OF PLANT AND ANIMAL LIFE. THE VASTNESS OF THESE LANDSCAPES IS BREATHTAKING, MATCHED BY THE PRODIGIOUS POPULATIONS OF SPECIALISED ANIMALS THAT LIVE IN THEM. HERDS OF CARIBOU AND WILDEBEEST, SWARMS OF MOSQUITOES — THE NUMBERS RANK IN MILLIONS. YET EVEN HERE THERE IS AN INTIMATE RELATIONSHIP OF CHECKS AND BALANCES THAT DICTATES WHICH SPECIES MERITS A NICHE IN A FINELY TUNED ECOSYSTEM.

TUNDRA GRAZER *A North American Dall's sheep.*

OCEANS OF GRASS

Grass is one of the most nutritious of plants. Across the globe

it dominates broad areas of the landscape and provides the

wherewithal for a trio of animal groups – burrowers, grazers

and carnivore predators – which exist on every continent.

In the rare surviving tallgrass prairies of the Midwest of the USA, big bluestem grass lives up to the prairies' name. Bluestem grass can grow to a height of 12 ft (3.7 m). If allowed to, it would naturally dominate the landscape, especially when rival plants are killed off by periodic prairie fires. Nothing, besides humankind, can compete with this sort of domination.

In the steppes of Kazakhstan – where they are not turned over to grain farming or horse herding – open grasslands present a similar scene. They roll on and on over the undulating landscape. Beneath the scudding clouds, waves ripple through the tall grasses, bent before the hushed breath of the wind, like a vast bronze-green sea.

The very vastness of the world's open grasslands – whether in the Great Plains of North America, Kazakhstan, Argentina or Mongolia – is breathtaking. When bathed in sunlight and filled with the smell of warm grasses, they have a refreshing simplicity. The contours of the landscape are softened; colours are reduced to a restricted palette of the blue in the sky, the white of clouds and the seas of green in subtly mutating shades, often turning to golden yellow as the summer progresses. There is a starkness, too, in a

SUMMER FLOURISH *False lupins (or lupines) throw a yellow shimmer over the Craters of the Moon National Monument in Idaho.*

scene where roads, if they exist at all, may stretch in straight lines from horizon to horizon; where there are few landmarks and the location and shape of towns and settlements can seem arbitrary and undisciplined. Winters are often long and grey, and, in summer, oppressive weather may set in for days on end, draining the landscape of colour. Eventually the mounting tension that accompanies rising atmospheric pressure is relieved by a thunderstorm, when dozens of rods of lightning arc between low clouds and earth, seeking out the rare features that rise above the plain.

Grasslands are newcomers. They developed only about 25 million years ago, in tandem with the rise of mammals. Now they are found on all the continents bar Antarctica, from the Equator to temperate zones, and account for 25 per cent of the Earth's land area – though much of them has been taken over for farming. In East Africa they are called the savannah, in South Africa the veldt, in Argentina the pampas, in Brazil the campos, in Venezuela and Colombia the llanos, in North America the prairies, in Central Asia the steppes.

Humans have a special interest in grass. Directly and indirectly, it forms the basis of the diet of virtually the entire race. Wheat, barley, millet, rice and maize are all kinds of grass and all are primary staple foods. Humans have always cast a covetous eye on grasslands, as places where such productive cereals can be grown – or food produced through grass-eating livestock. Grasslands have been under threat since humans became agriculturalists 10 000 years ago.

Natural grasslands are immensely productive. They can produce over 5000 lb of forage per acre (1 tonne per hectare) in a year, and can support a greater weight of animals per acre than any other habitat. Grass not only tolerates grazing, it thrives on it – regenerating profusely after cropping from growing points close to the ground.

Grass in its raw state is not easy to digest – but one group of animals has made it a speciality. These are the ruminants, such as cattle, goats, sheep, antelopes and camels. They extract the maximum nutritional value from grass through a complex process of digestion. First, the grass is chewed, chopped into pieces and dispatched to a chamber called the rumen, where bacteria and protozoans break it down. It is then returned to the animal's mouth, where it is chewed further as cud. It later passes through one or two further stomachs before reaching the abomascum, where the proteins are extracted by digestive juices.

BALANCING ACT

The North American prairies are home to some 400 different species of plants. These have to be specialists to survive the swamping effect of grass. They tend to have bulbs or bulbous roots which store water in competition with the gluttonous water uptake of the grass, and

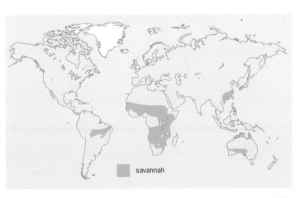

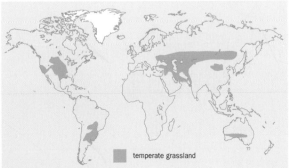

WHERE GRASS RULES *Savannah (above left) covers large swathes of the tropics. Temperate grasslands or steppes (left) spread across central Europe and Asia and the Americas.*

COLOUR FIELDS *Bluebonnets and scarlet paintbrush flowers transform the Texas prairies into a riot of spring colour.*

which can survive the fires that regularly sweep across the plains. They also have to tolerate or repulse grazing animals. Those that fulfil these criteria are often flowering plants, with the result that all grasslands are seasonally speckled with spectacular flowers, such as gladioli, orchids and hyacinths. Tall plants such as cornflowers and poppies also do well: they can compete for light with the grasses and contain comparatively little sap, so need only moderate amounts of water.

Grasslands vary in climate, and in the species they support, but all have much in common. Rainfall is a key factor. Grass demands only that there is enough rain in the growing season to see it through its cycle. In warm countries, the rainfall on grasslands may last for just one season, perhaps three or four months long, but this is enough. Any more would encourage the growth of the grasslands' rival, woodland. Any less rain would result in desert. It is a fine balance.

Its delicacy was demonstrated in the 1930s, when the prairie lands of much of the central southern USA were reduced to a parched semi-desert, the Dustbowl. Despite warnings about the appropriate use of land, the prairies of central North America had been subjected to continual encroachment by farmers and ranchers from the mid 19th century onwards.

The soil, of a kind known as *loess*, was a fragile mix of clay and silt that once lay beneath a great inland sea. It was densely packed, and held in place, with the miles of roots that were the key to grass's success: it was often iron-hard, and the pioneers who had the task of breaking it up for arable farming earned the name 'sodbusters'. In the 1930s a series of dry years showed the true ecological damage inflicted by ploughing, overgrazing and the trampling

PRAIRIE SPECIALISTS *With their heads down and branched horns lowered, pronghorn antelopes graze the prairie grasslands.*

of introduced cattle. First in Oklahoma and Texas, then in neighbouring states, the fields turned to dust: the topsoil, now broken up, was literally blown away. Many of the farmers were ruined.

PRAIRIE GLORY

The North American prairies once stretched from Texas to Alberta, from the Rockies to Ohio. Here was a grassland of breathtaking immensity – the biggest on Earth. It was inhabited by millions of pronghorns, ruminants related to antelopes with unusual branched horns, and billions of prairie dogs, a kind of ground squirrel. But the prairies' true ruler was the bison (or buffalo), which numbered tens of millions. To the new settlers, however, these animals were either game to be exploited or a nuisance to be removed, so that the true commercial potential of the grasslands could be realised.

In fact, there were three grasslands in the prairies. In the rain shadow of the Rockies, where rainfall was lowest, lay the short-grass prairies with drought-tolerant grasses such as buffalo grass and blue grama. On the wetter eastern margins were the tallgrass prairies, dominated by the big bluestem, Indian grass and switchgrass; in between lay mixed-grass prairies.

BUBBLE NECK *The North American prairie chicken is, in fact, a kind of grouse noted for the inflatable neck sacs that produce its booming call.*

THE FALL AND RISE OF THE BISON

In 1806, the explorers Meriwether Lewis and William Clark led a 'Corps of Discovery' through South Dakota on the first official expedition across North America. Among the most awesome sights they encountered were the bison: vast herds on the move, stretching as far as the eye could see, filling the air with a deep rumble. 'The moving multitude . . . darkened the whole plain', they reported later.

Bison – also referred to as buffalo, because of their family resemblance to Asian and African buffalo – were the archetypal big grazers of the North American prairies. With their thick coats and robust physique they can withstand the icy blasts of winter, and yet in a burst of speed they can run as fast as a horse. They live for 20 years or more, and the females produce one calf each year after the age of three. They are the largest mammals of North America – adult males stand 6^{1}/$_{2}$ft (2 m) at the shoulder and weigh about a ton.

At the time of Lewis and Clark's expedition, an estimated 70 million bison roamed the American prairies – a biomass equivalent to the entire human population of the USA and Canada today. They moved around in large herds, migrating south in the autumn. Some migrating herds were so large that they took five days to pass a fixed point. By 1895 fewer than 1000 remained.

The Plains Indians, such as the Sioux, Cheyenne and Comanche, developed a whole culture around the bison, picking off enough of them to serve their modest needs. Bison provided them with meat, skins to make tepees and moccasin soles, sinews for bowstrings, and bones for tools and weapons.

When East Coast Americans expanded westwards in the wake of the Lewis and Clark expedition, they began to see the potential of bison as a provider. To a man with a rifle the bison were easy prey – and they appeared to be a limitless resource. When the railroads were built across America in the 1860s the slaughter of bison gathered pace. Hunters could kill dozens in a day, and load their bodies onto the railway wagons for processing back in the eastern cities, such as Detroit. They were killed for meat, for their hides and for sport. 'Buffalo Bill' Cody, founder of the famous Wild West Show, claimed to have killed 4000 in 18 months when he was hunting to feed the railway gangs. There was little attempt to exploit carcasses to the full. Often they were stripped of their hides and tongues (considered a delicacy) and then abandoned. Soon the Great Plains were a graveyard of carcasses.

There was another motive behind the slaughter. The Plains Indians got in the way of the new settlers of the West, and frictions had resulted in a prolonged Indian War, punctuated by atrocities on both sides. In 1876 Representative James Throckmorton of Texas declared: 'I believe it would be a great step forward in the civilisation of the Indians and the preservation of peace . . . if there was not a buffalo in existence.' The logic was simple: destroy the bison, and destroy the Indian way of life.

By the 1880s the strategy had more or less worked. The bison populations had been drastically reduced and the Plains Indians were in crisis. Many reluctantly opted to live on the reservations set aside for them. The settlers moved onto the plains, carving up the land into farms and introducing their own form of cattle onto their ranches.

The bison is no longer threatened by extinction. There are now some 200 000 of them, in scattered herds on various private ranches and in public parks such as the Wind Cave National Park in South Dakota and Yellowstone in Wyoming. But without the freedom to migrate and roam the prairies, the true glory of the bison herds can only be imagined.

BUFFALO ROAMING *Once close to extinction, bison (or buffalo) are rebuilding their numbers in parks and ranches.*

The tall-grass prairies have now all but disappeared beneath the cornbelt of Illinois, Iowa and Missouri. The mixed and short-grass prairies have been severely depleted. Only 3 per cent of the total has never been put to the plough. But natural prairies have always had their devotees, and pockets have survived in their original state and are now preserved – especially in regions where agriculture was always going to be difficult, such as the Flint Hills of Kansas and the Sand Hills of Nebraska.

In such places it is still possible to see what the prairies once meant. Herds of bison and pronghorn graze on the open hillsides. Short-tailed shrews and grasshopper mice scamper under foot, pursued by ferruginous hawks. With a wingspan of 5 ft (1.5 m), the ferruginous hawk – so named after its rusty brown colour, from the Latin *ferrum*, 'iron' – is the largest North American hawk. In the absence of trees, it nests on the ground, as do horned larks and prairie chickens – famous for their noisy mating displays when the males create deep booming sounds and inflate their vivid pink cheek sacs.

Horned larks reveal another adaptation which the open prairie has imposed upon them: females are often seen limping away from their nests, as if with a broken wing, in a cunning ploy to distract predators from their vulnerable young. Once the enemy has been lured off the scent of her young, the mother bird will fly away.

The prairies' main predators are bobcats (lynxes), cougars and coyotes, playing their own self-appointed role in maintaining the genetic strength of the prairie animals by picking off the sick and the weak.

Ever on the lookout, prairie dogs mount guards around their burrows and yap signals to each other as they go about their daily business collecting seeds and cropping grass. These highly social animals congregate in huge groups, known as 'towns', if their populations grow unchecked. In 1901 one town in Texas covered an area twice the size of Wales and was estimated to contain 400 million prairie dogs. The larger towns were thought to be centuries old. But the new settlers and ranchers of the West in the late 19th and early 20th centuries had no place for prairie dogs: they ate the grass and their concealed tunnels tended to injure horses. They were subjected to a prolonged campaign of extermination during which 90 per cent of their population was obliterated. Now their place in the ecosystem is better appreciated: their burrowing helps to maintain much of the diversity of the prairie ecology.

ICE AGE PONDS *Blocks of ice embedded in the soil after the glaciers of the last Ice Age had withdrawn created the pothole landscape of North Dakota.*

THE CHOCOLATE HILLS OF BOHOL

One of the strangest grasslands is found on the small island of Bohol in the Philippines. More than 1200 evenly rounded hills, each 100-300 ft (30-100 m) high, lie stretched across some 20 sq miles (50 km²), looking rather like the inside of a giant egg box. No one knows exactly how they were formed: the hills are mainly limestone and may have been shaped simply by centuries of evenly distributed weathering. The local people, however, have their own more romantic version. They say that the hills are the teardrops of a mythical giant who was spurned by

GOING CHOCOLATE *The flanks of the Bohol hills turn brown as the dry season advances.*

a mortal girl with whom he had fallen hopelessly in love.

For much of the year the hills are covered in a deep and thick layer of long, emerald-green grass, watered by the copious tropical rains. But

under the relentless heat of the dry season, which begins in February and lasts until May, the grasses dry out and turn brown, giving rise to the popular name for this geological oddity: the Chocolate Hills of Bohol.

They provide homes for squatters, such as burrowing owls, prairie voles and rattlesnakes; and by cropping the grass they promote the diversity of prairie plants.

Grasshoppers are in their element on the prairies – sometimes expanding to plague proportions – while brightly coloured butterflies such as satyrs, red admirals and sulfurs dart among the flowers. On the ground are dung beetles busy around the cropped grass, burying the balls of animal droppings in which they lay their eggs. Gophers and moles burrow underground, where they cannot avoid encountering huge numbers of earthworms. It is said that, weight for weight, the earthworms beneath the prairie grass match the grazers above.

Pockets of alternative habitats provide for a greater diversity of life than the seas of grass are able to support. Stands of trees, such as cottonwoods and ash, line the rivers, creating islands of shade and perches for migrating birds. In days of old, bison assembled in huge numbers around waterholes, wallowing in the mud to ward off mosquitoes, and churning up the surrounding soil to form an enlarged bowl. These 'buffalo wallows' still fill with rainwater, and provide stop-off points for geese, ducks and cranes. More significant are the potholes of North Dakota, a pitted landscape created by retreating glaciers at the end of the last Ice Age. Hundreds of ponds dot the landscape, providing a breeding ground for half of all of North America's ducks.

GRAZER, BURROWER, PREDATOR

At the hub of the ecology of the great grasslands are the grazers, burrowers, and predators. On the Central Asian steppes, stretching from the Black Sea to the Altai Mountains on the borders of China, Russia and Mongolia, the big grazers are saiga, stocky sheep-like antelopes with strange

LARGEST RODENT *Capybaras are sociable creatures. At dawn and dusk, they often gather to feed in groups at the waterside.*

noses like foreshortened trunks. The burrowers are ground squirrels called susliks, marmots, hamsters and blind mole rats – the world's best burrowers, digging tunnels that can be 1200 ft (400 m) long. Here the main predators swoop down from the air: imperial eagles, steppe eagles and great bustards. The other great bird of the steppes is the demoiselle crane, which, after elaborate courtship dances, nests in shallow 'scrapes' – bowl-like scoops in the ground – before migrating to Africa for the winter.

On the campos and pampas of South America, cavies – a kind of outsized guinea pig – and burrowing viscachas crop the grass, while caracara hawks, pampas foxes and long-legged maned wolves act as the chief predators. More specialist animals have carved out niches, such as the armadillo and the giant anteater, both of which live mainly by foraging for termites in huge underground nests. Surprisingly perhaps, the largest herbivore here is not a mammal but a bird. The rhea is a flightless bird similar to, but smaller than, the ostrich.

One of the most common birds of the pampas is the spur-winged plover which has adopted the same tactic as the horned lark in the North American prairies. It diverts attention from its nest by crying plaintively and pretending to be injured.

The wetter llano grasslands farther north, in Venezuela and Colombia, are home to the biggest of all rodents, the capybara, which can grow up to 4 ft (1.3 m) in length. Capybaras tend to live near waterways, and their diet consists mainly of aquatic plants and grasses. With their sense organs on the top of their heads, they can rest in shallow water like hippos.

In Australia, the dominant herbivores of the dry grasslands and mulga scrub are kangaroos and wallabies, but emus and burrowing wombats also play their part. Here, as in dry grasslands everywhere, fire is always a threat. The kangaroo is one of the few animals that can delay the development of the embryo, advisable if a fire has made food scarce. The female can hold the embryo in suspension (diapause) for about a year before releasing it into her pouch. Kangaroos are otherwise highly productive: a mother usually has an infant on the ground, a joey in her pouch and an embryo on the way.

THE GREATEST GRASSLANDS

Nowhere is the grassland pattern of grazer, predator and burrower more superbly displayed than in the grasslands of East Africa. Preserved from ranching by the tsetse fly, which causes sleeping sickness in domestic

STEPPE BEAUTIES *Demoiselle cranes forage for insects and other small animals as well as roots, fruits and seeds.*

livestock and humans, these grasslands are home to the world's richest collection of large mammals. Here the main herbivores are zebras, gazelles and antelopes, wildebeest and buffaloes. They are preyed upon by some of the most skilled predators of the animal kingdom, such as lions, cheetahs, leopards and hyenas. Hyenas were once thought to be primarily scavengers, but have now been shown to be courageous

SOLITARY MOMENT *In the bright midsummer sunlight of South Africa, the zebra's stripes offer little camouflage.*

BREEDING MACHINE *The body of a fertile queen termite is little more than a large, egg-filled sac.*

hunters, working in packs under the cover of darkness. The greatest of the true scavengers is the vulture. It can spot a carcass from a great distance, and its specially denuded head allows it to reach well into a rib cage with the minimum of mess.

Hunters and the hunted have to blend into the background. Most of the animals of the African grasslands are the colour of dry-season grass, protecting them at the time when the stakes are highest. Some animals also have diversionary camouflage. The rear end of a bushbuck flashes white as it darts away, confusing a predator's sense of direction and distance. The purpose of the zebra's striking coloration, however, remains a mystery. Is it designed to confuse the eye in the chase, or is it effective camouflage at dusk and night, when predators are at their most active? Or is it that, like many of the other grassland herbivores, a zebra's safety is in numbers, and camouflage comes low on its list of evolutionary priorities?

To several herbivores of the African grasslands, their protection from predators

is vested in their sheer size. Elephants move about in small herds, pulling up tussocks of grass and even young trees with their trunks. Rhinoceroses are solitary creatures, coming together only for mating, otherwise living

WORKBENCH OF EVOLUTION

Key moments of human evolution seem to have coincided with climate change, when colder, drier conditions favoured grassland. Such change puts stress on animal species. Our ancestors being agile and able to run upright, to eat a range of foods and develop the use of tools, were well able to meet this challenge – even though their ancestors were almost certainly rain-forest creatures. The development of grassland appears to have had a crucial impact on the way we evolved.

out their lives on the edges of herds of other grazers. Giraffes are adapted to feed off the tops of trees. They are in part responsible for the box-like shape of the acacia trees that dot these grasslands, while the undersides of the trees are cropped by gerenuk antelopes standing on their hind legs.

Pressure from grazers has prompted one type of acacia to develop a relationship

with an ant, a classic example of interdependence to mutual advantage known as symbiosis. This species of ant, cremato-gaster, builds its home in galls on the tips of the branches, and lives in the protection of the tree's sharp thorns. Giraffes have tough mouths that can cope with these thorns – but they do not like the sting the ants can deliver. So in lieu of rent, the ant provides protection. These acacias are known as whistling thorns, because of the low whistling sound created as the breeze passes over the tiny holes in the galls.

Another case of symbiosis is the relationship between oxpeckers and large grazers, such as buffaloes, rhinoceroses and elands. Oxpeckers, members of the starling family, sit on the body of their hosts and peck off blood-gorged ticks and other parasites. They also act as early warning systems, flying off when danger is spotted.

The greatest earthmovers of the grasslands are among the smallest: termites. At the centre of their complex societies lies an utter dependency on fungus. These relatives of cockroaches live in vast colonies strictly divided into hierarchies based on job description. The future of young termites is somehow determined at an early age, and they are transformed as adults into the appropriate body form – whether as worker, soldier, builder or nurse. At the pinnacle of the hierarchy is the queen, whose

WILDEBEEST ON THE MOVE

First come the zebras, then the wildebeest, and then the hartebeest and gazelles bring up the rear. Every year, as the Serengeti plains in northern Tanzania begin to frazzle beneath the dry-season sun, the great herds set off on their annual migration, travelling some 500 miles (800 km) in a sweeping clockwise procession in search of green pasture.

The dry season begins in May, striking the south-eastern part of the plains first. Zebra, which prefer longer grass, gather and move off, heading north-west. Wildebeest prefer medium-length grass, but before long this too is depleted. It triggers one of the most impressive sights of Africa: about 1 million wildebeest on the move. When they reach rivers, the sheer force of numbers pushes them on, forcing them to leap down high banks and wade and swim across the torrents. Panic results in stampedes, and many of the animals are drowned. This frenzied activity coincides with the rutting season.

In June the herds reach the north-west sector of the plain, and during July and August they move on farther, crossing the border into the Mara region of southern Kenya. In

NO TURNING BACK *Wildebeest have to ford several rivers in their migratory route, notably the Mara, which flows into Lake Victoria.*

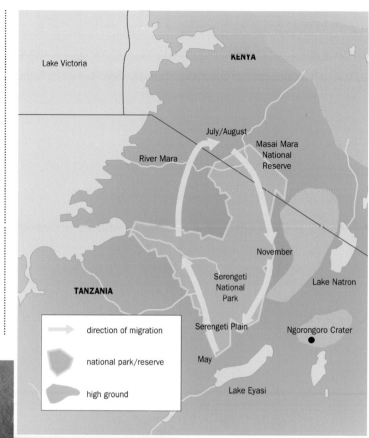

CIRCLE OF LIFE *Wildebeests' elliptical progression takes them through grasslands and thorn-tree woodlands.*

November the dry season reaches the north-west, but now the wet season is beginning in the south-east. The herds continue their tour. Back in the south once more, the young wildebeest are born. Miraculously almost all the females give birth within a few days of each other, allowing the herd to stick together and shelter in the safety of numbers from the predations of ever-present hyenas and lions.

sole function is to produce thousands of eggs out of her bag-like body – some 30 000 every day for 20 years.

Termites feed off plant material, notably grass – indeed they probably consume more grass than all the large mammals put together. But they cannot digest the cellulose unless it is broken down by fungus. Their mounds are built out of chewed mud hardened by saliva, and contain a network of tunnels and chambers, as well as chimneys for ventilation. They may house as many as 2 million insects and rise 23 ft (7 m) high. At the heart of the mound is the food chamber, where food is collected and then exposed to the fungus, which will render it digestible. Food parcels are then distributed throughout the colony. Saliva passed with this food may also carry the signals which control the colony, and make it act almost as if it were a single organism.

WASTELANDS, BADLANDS AND TUNDRA

The tundra remains one of the world's largest undisturbed natural habitats, a harsh environment, where only specialised plants and animals can survive. Even greater challenges to life are posed by the places dismissed as wastelands and badlands.

Flat and endless beneath a slate-grey sky for most of the year, the tundra presents a desolate picture. Icy Arctic winds chase over the treeless horizon in autumn, bringing flurries of snow spiked with ice particles, and gripping the land with frost. Broad, shallow rivers edged with ice slide down the inclines, splitting into silvery braids between strands of gravel and low islands. As winter sets in and temperatures plummet to –44°C (–47°F), the ground freezes like iron, and the sedges and heathers turn black in the pale light of the ever-shortening days, before succumbing to the whiteout of heavy snow. Caribou move across the landscape, heads down against the wind, their trails emphasising the vast scale of the landscape.

The tundra is one of the world's largest habitats, stretching in a giant hoop around most of the northern crown of the globe, from Scandinavia, across Siberia and Alaska, to the east coast of Canada. It is hemmed in by the shores of the Arctic in the north and by the taiga, the band of conifer forests that lies to the south. The tundra is constantly under stress, freezing, thawing, expanding and contracting. Repeated time and again this process

WET SUMMER *The tundra is dotted with pools of water, trapped by the waterlogged soil and the permafrost beneath.*

HIGH RISE *North America's highest peak, Mount McKinley (above), rises from the Alaskan tundra. Lichens (right) cover rocks with the characteristic tweedy colours of the tundra.*

has shaped the very look of the landscape. The push and pull of ice and glaciers has scoured and flattened the land, grinding boulders into shattered debris and gravel.

A LANDSCAPE WITHOUT TREES

The absence of trees is part of the definition of tundra. Trees cannot tolerate the wind and cold and the truncated growing season of the northern summer. But most of all they cannot tolerate the permafrost. About 3 ft (1 m) on average beneath the surface of the tundra, the soil is permanently frozen, winter and summer. In summer the sun melts the topsoil, but the farther north one

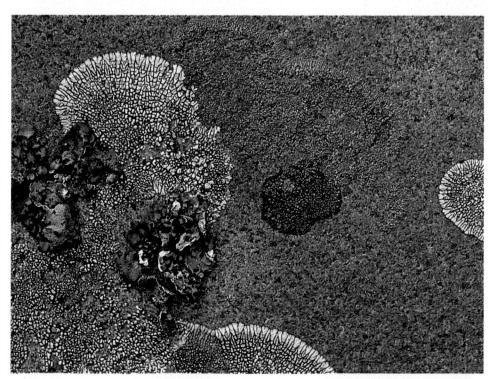

goes, the shallower the sun's penetration. This sun-softened upper layer of tundra soil rapidly turns into a soggy, waterlogged mass. Full-size trees cannot take root here – although dwarf varieties, such as dwarf birch and dwarf willow appear, lying flat against the ground to take shelter in winter beneath an insulating layer of snow. Only much farther south do they begin to stand upright, at first squatting low like shrubs, shaped like tattered flags by the prevailing winds.

The most characteristic tundra plants are tough, ground-hugging and compact. They can cope with the cold and the oxygen-starved sogginess of their habitat. Grass-like sedges grow in clumps, sometimes forming large areas of tussocky bumps. Grasses, heathers and mosses take hold where they can, as well as the spongy, tall-growing lichen, *Cladonia rangiferina*. In winter caribou paw away at the snow and ice to reach

this lichen, a staple food that has earnt the name 'caribou moss'.

Only a few animals inhabit the tundra permanently. Caribou – called reindeer in Scandinavia and Siberia – roam across it, escaping the worst of the winter by migrating south to the northern margins of the taiga. Ptarmigan, snowy owls, Arctic foxes and Arctic wolves survive in their white winter clothes.

In the three or four months into which spring, summer and autumn are shoehorned, the tundra bursts magically into

CAMOUFLAGE *An Arctic fox's summer coat stands out against tundra flowers, but would be hard to pick out against a background of bare rock.*

FULL SUMMER *August brings flowers to the Alaskan tundra. These plants depend upon the resilience of their roots to survive from year to year.*

BADLANDS AND TRADERS

The tundra remains one of the world's least disturbed habitats. Humans have little tolerance for the conditions that prevail there. Trappers and hunters venture into it in pursuit of seasonal game, but their permanent settlements tend to lie well to the south.

There are many other places in the world which have been similarly dismissed by humans as useless wastelands – and many of them with some justice. Their inhospitable character is at once fearsome and awe-inspiring. Much of the Gobi Desert of Mongolia and northern China is a hostile world of blistering summers and freezing winters, visited only by passing trading caravans supported by the endurance of Bactrian camels. Farther west, the ancient Silk Road skirts the Taklimakan Desert, which has the reputation of being one of the most desolate and deadly tracts of land in the world. Its name means 'You enter and never return'.

In the prairies of the American West, there are a number of areas where low rainfall and soft, sedimentary rock have combined to create terrains that have no conceivable use to humans. They cannot be harnessed for agriculture, and many are too rugged even to cross. They are 'Badlands'.

Several of these are so magnificently eroded, however, that they have become objects of wonder. The Badlands of South Dakota have degenerated over 5 million years into a labyrinth of shifting mounds. Yet even here, plants and animals can find a niche. Bison and pronghorn

BADLANDS Mako sika *was the Sioux Indian name for this kind of country in South Dakota – 'bad lands': bad to cross, bad to be lost in.*

antelopes graze on prairie grass growing on the flat table-top summits. Bats and rattlesnakes inhabit the caves, and birds feed on chokeberry bushes that line the gullies. Bryce Canyon in Utah presents an even more dramatically eroded landscape. Among the strange and mysterious clusters of spires, pinnacles and buttresses, trees grow up next to the canyon walls, while ancient bristlecone pines cling to the higher slopes, and marmots dart among the rocks.

To make a landscape yet more desolate, add salt. There are few more challenging environments than salt flats – and few more inhospitable than the Karum Salt Flats of eastern Ethiopia and Eritrea. Once this land, part of the Danakil Depression, lay beneath a shallow inlet of the Red Sea and over the millennia salt accumulated here in vast quantities. Today the salt deposits are thought to be 3 miles (5 km) deep. The surface lies 400 ft (122 m) below sea level, encrusted in white salt like an Arctic waste. The lowest points are briefly turned into a shallow, briny lake, stained

SALT LICK *Encrustations of salt look strangely like snow as camels slake their thirst in one of the lowest places on Earth, the flat basin of Lake Assal in the Great Rift Valley.*

red with iron oxide, as water rushes off neighbouring mountains after the rainy season.

The Danakil Depression lies in the Great Rift Valley, beneath the lava-strewn volcanoes of Erta Alé that indicate the continued subterranean stress along this faultline. Here and there on the salt flats steam from volcanic fumaroles pushes up fragile, crusty domes of brown salt, over pools of boiling brine. In the wet season salt-laden ground water emerges onto the surface; it spills into pools where the heat of the searing sun concentrates the mineral content and turns the water into a range of bright, unearthly colours. This is a true wasteland – and only the Earth's most adaptable creatures could begin to tolerate it. Yet in the midst of the Karum Salt Flats there is indeed some life: people making a living by digging out the salt.

MAMMOTHS IN THE DEEP FREEZE

Until about 12 000 years ago, a broad range of animals roamed the open spaces of the Northern Hemisphere now occupied by the tundra. Many are now extinct, such as an early form of camel, the giant ground sloth, the woolly rhinoceros, the great American short-faced bear and the sabre-toothed cat. Perhaps the best known is the giant of the cold north, the woolly mammoth.

In their heyday, the populations of mammoths probably numbered several million. They roamed from northern Europe to Siberia and North America, where conditions at the waning of the Ice Age were generally colder than they are today. It is in the ice-bound wastes of northern Siberia that the most remarkable mammoth finds have come to light.

At some remote moment of the past, a number of mammoths died by falling into sinkholes or by becoming trapped in a mudflow or semifrozen marshes. Buried by layers of ice and solifluction, they became a part of the permafrost – frozen, desiccated, but otherwise preserved in a near-perfect state.

In northern Siberia the heat of the summer sun thaws the exposed surface of the permafrost. Where a river is carving out its banks into the permafrost, fresh layers are exposed to the sun each year. Similarly, gold-miners use jets of water to thaw the soil on exposed faces, so that the earth can be sieved. Every now and then, a body will appear as the permafrost is pushed back – a mammoth out of the deep freeze.

Some of these bodies have been perfectly preserved, such as 'Dima', the 40 000-year-old body of a baby mammoth found in 1976. Others have been partially decayed, or gnawed by scavenging animals, either at the time of death or after the body has thawed and lain undiscovered. When alerted to a find, specialist scientists have to move fast to rescue the body from decay, and this process often begins with long and gruelling journeys into extremely remote regions. Nonetheless, several skeletons, complete with tusks and samples of skin, hair and internal organs have been retrieved and preserved, giving researchers a very thorough insight into the nature and habits of the mammoth, such as the precise nature of its diet.

Mammoth research has become more difficult in recent years. Scientific expeditions are expensive to mount and logistically tricky – and mammoths have become an ever lower priority under the economic constraints of post-Communist Russia. Many goldminers also view the discovery of a mammoth as a nuisance that can cause prolonged delays to their work while a scientific team is summoned and carries out its painstaking investigation. Only too often they succumb to the temptation to bury their find and keep quiet.

IN THEIR ELEMENT *Shaggy mats of dense fur protected mammoths from the cold.*

life. Now the days are long, and the sun barely sets, transforming the landscape into a soft and soggy world dappled with ponds and lakes that lie like the scattered shards of a broken mirror. As temperatures rise to 5°C (40°F) or more, the tundra's sober-hued winter cloak becomes speckled with extravagant highlights of colour as the flowers burst into bloom. Poppies spring up to produce orange and yellow flowers, their delicate stems covered with fine hairs to conserve the warmth. Lupins produce towering heads of purple and mauve flowers, rivalled only by fireweed and the showy bell-shaped flowers of monkshood, while, low on the ground, saxifrage and campion push up nodding clusters of white and pink flowers from their compact mats of foliage. The dwarf shrubs also come into bloom, such as azaleas and Lapland rosebay, a form of rhododendron.

Butterflies, moths, spiders and crane-flies busy themselves among the freshly laid carpet of growth. Less welcome, but very much a part of tundra life, are the midges and mosquitoes – billions of them. Female mosquitoes need the protein of fresh blood to lay their eggs, so they hound the caribou and other vertebrates mercilessly.

This rich flurry of life attracts many summer visitors to the tundra – especially migrating birds, which arrive by the millions to breed. For them, the summer tundra presents a safe and remote haven, where food is readily available to feed their young. Snow geese, swans, barnacle geese, red-necked phalaropes, plovers, sandpipers, pintail ducks, teal and many others fly in from all over the world. Fish, such as the Arctic char, move upstream and into lakes freed from the grip of ice.

As the birds, caribou, hares and lemmings tend to their young, the predators,

KING OF ALL HE SURVEYS Male caribou – or reindeer – reach prime condition in late summer. The male's antlers are much larger than the female's.

such as lynxes and grey wolves move in. They play an important part in population control. Cycles of boom and bust are a regular part of tundra life. Every four years or so populations of caribou or horseshoe hares reach a critical level, after which the feeding resources become overstrained, causing the populations to go into decline. The populations of predators, such as grey wolves and Alaskan red foxes, mirror this cycle, but with a delay of a year. When their prey is numerous, they have plenty to eat. Times are good and their populations expand, but then their prey goes into decline and times become hard for the now-expanded predator population. They are weakened – which in turn gives the prey the opportunity to expand once more.

Lemmings, vole-like rodents about 4-7 in (10-18 cm) long, are famous for the way

SEEDS IN COLD STORAGE

The seeds of the the tundra's various flowering plants have been shown to have an extraordinary resilience. It appears that lupin seeds, for example, can remain viable in the permafrost for thousands of years: seeds taken from 10 000-year-old permafrost have successfully germinated. However, the summer is too short to rely on propagation by seed. As a result, most tundra plants are hardy perennials, and new shoots grow from the roots.

they regulate their own populations. These burrowing creatures can reproduce at a fantastic rate in times of glut. When overpopulation creates a food crisis, lemmings

PLENTIFUL FARE Close to the ground, the Alaskan tundra is a dense mat of lichens, mosses and berries in autumn – rich pickings for grazing animals.

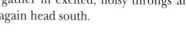

migrate en masse in search of better pickings. They generally follow tracks already beaten by people or other animals, and wherever possible try to avoid water crossings. However, the urge to migrate, combined with pressure from predators pursuing them, has on occasion forced large columns to take unwise routes over precipices and through rivers, resulting in widespread deaths. This phenomenon has in the past been mistakenly interpreted as mass suicide.

Autumn comes early and very swiftly to the tundra, cloaking it in the soft, tweedy colours of heather flowers and the rich reds and oranges of the fruit and leaves of the zone's many berry-bearing shrubs, such as

cloudberry, bearberry and crowberry. As the first early flakes of snow blow in, the birds gather in excited, noisy throngs and once again head south.

POLYGONS AND PINGOS

Cold and ice define the landscape of the tundra. In Siberia the soil is frozen to a depth of 4500 ft (1370 m), and has been for more than a million years. In summer, gluey layers of water-saturated surface soil on slopes sometimes slide gently downhill – a

CRATER OF ICE *A pingo on the Mackenzie River in northern Canada has a typically volcano-like appearance.*

process known as solifluction, from the Latin *solum*, 'ground' or 'earth', and *fluere*, 'to move'.

Across many of the wetter regions of the tundra, freezing water in winter pushes away rocks and gravel, creating rims around ponds and lakes. Over large areas the ice and rims clamp together under the stress of contracting soil and expanding water. The result is a honeycomb of lakes and pools known as polygonal tundra. In some places, a similar effect is produced in miniature by rocks standing on gravel. In the summer, when the ice has melted away, the rocks stand proud in a network of linked circles.

Where water or a pool of water-saturated silt is trapped by encircling permafrost, a pingo may form. Pingos are ice hills, covered in a thin layer of soil and vegetation, and may be the highest landmark for many miles around. At the very pinnacle a pond will form, like the crater of a volcano. With the gradual accumulation of more water, and continued pressure from the permafrost, pingos grow constantly over the years, but at some point the structure becomes unsustainable: the ice cracks and the pingo slowly collapses. The largest, at Ibyuk in the Northwest Territories of Canada, rises to 157 ft (48 m), and

WEB OF PONDS *A ceaseless round of thawing and freezing produces polygonal tundra in a waterlogged, flat landscape.*

is probably approaching the limit of growth after about 1000 years.

Not all the tundra is frozen and soggy. Sand dunes line part of the Kobuk River in north-west Alaska, a remnant of the last Ice Age. Across northern Alaska lies the Brooks Range rising to 9060 ft (2761 m) at Mount Isto. The height of the mountains creates its own climate and sustains a broader range of animals than the open tundra. Moose and Dall's sheep, with magnificent curling horns, migrate in summer from the south of the mountains to their breeding grounds on the northern slopes, while lynxes and Alaskan red foxes seek out their prey, such as burrowing pikas, and grizzly bears search for berries, bulbs and carrion among the shrubs and rivers on the lowland slopes.

WATER WORLDS 5

LIFE ON EARTH BEGAN IN WATER, AND WATER OCCUPIES MORE THAN TWO-THIRDS OF THE EARTH'S SURFACE — AND YET IT IS THE HABITAT TO WHICH HUMANS ARE LEAST WELL ADAPTED. WE CANNOT BREATHE IN IT UNAIDED OR COPE WITH THE PRESSURES OF GREAT DEPTHS. HERE WE ARE TRULY ALIEN INTRUDERS. KNOWLEDGE OF THE WORLD OF WATER, OF THE DEEPEST LAKES, SEAS AND OCEANS, HAS GROWN OVER THE PAST FEW DECADES, AS UNDERWATER EXPLORATION HAS BEEN MADE POSSIBLE WITH DEVELOPING TECHNOLOGY — BUT IT REMAINS COMPARATIVELY UNFAMILIAR. IT IS A VAST AND MYSTERIOUS WORLD OF EXTRAORDINARY BEAUTY — AND A WORLD WHICH HAS YET TO YIELD MANY OF ITS WONDERS AND SECRETS.

THE CAULDRON OF LIFE

Hot water, steam and boiling mud bubbling up from deep beneath the ground are reminders of the Earth's dynamic turbulence. They may also be the starting point of the most astounding creative endeavour in the Universe: life.

There is little to indicate the springs of Saturnia from afar. Signposts point across the agricultural landscape of southern Tuscany in Italy. Then, about half a mile (0.8 km) short of the village, there is a whiff of sulphur in the air – and there, open to the air and surrounded by fields, are the *terme*, a stairway of natural basins filled by hot water that pours out of the hillside from its volcanic source deep below the ground. Bathers pick their way among the steam-shrouded basins. They sink into the warm pools or lie in the torrents, letting themselves be pummelled by the gushing water. The springs of Saturnia were celebrated by the Romans, whose legends spoke of a city founded by the god Saturn. With their open, natural setting, they speak of times yet more remote. These springs have probably been cherished since the earliest humans came upon them.

Hot springs are laden with minerals, such as calcite, iron oxide, manganese, sulphates and nitrates. In tolerable quantities, they have long been considered beneficial to health. If left to its own devices, the calcite or lime creates the gently rounded basins over which the stilled water will brim. Some of the most impressive are found at the famous springs of Pamukkale in Turkey, which cover 300 acres (125 ha) in tier after tier of pristine white basins.

Rotorua on New Zealand's North Island lies at the heart of a large volcanically active region dotted with hot springs, steam vents and geysers. In the Waimangu thermal

HOT MISTS The hot lakes and pools of Waimangu in New Zealand produce a haze of drifting steam, which hangs in the valleys like dawn mists.

GREAT CASCADE The lime-laden water of Pamukkale in Turkey has built up the walls of thousands of shallow basins.

district the steep-sided, wooded valleys seem to be strangely filled with low clouds – like plugs of cotton wool – that have somehow become detached from the sky. This is steam rising from fissures in the rocks, and from pools and lakes of boiling water, such as The Cauldron. Elsewhere, usually from flat tables of bare rock, geysers gasp and produce pillars of steam and super-heated water. This is an area of great physical beauty, unearthly beneath its ever-changing veils of steam, and also strangely topsy-turvy. Lakes and pools elsewhere in the world are places of cool stillness; here, however, they strike a note of turbulence.

ARTISTS' PAINTPOTS

Feeding off the nutrient-rich water of hot springs, bacteria and algae combine to form mat-like scum. These can be poisonous to other life, and are sometimes unsightly – but they are also responsible for some of the beautiful colour effects in the pools that collect around hot springs – yellow, blue, red, emerald, turquoise. At Yellowstone Park in Wyoming, USA, these pools have earned poetic titles, such the Morning Glory Pool, the

WATER HEATER *Hot water in Yellowstone bubbles up from deep beneath the ground, tinted a variety of delicate hues by the minerals it carries.*

The patches of warmth have created microclimates amid the raw winter cold. Some vents and hot springs appear like jewelled islands, surrounded by damp green moss, ferns and tufts of grass. Here snails, frogs and a variety of insects pass the winter as if beneath the insulated dome of a heated swimming pool.

The same effect occurs in other cold areas – where the contrasts can be even more striking. The Nahanni River region in Canada's Northwest Territories spends eight months of the year under a veil of snow and ice, but at the Rabbitkettle Hotsprings boiling water emerges from the summit of a mound of lime deposit or tufa.

Artists' Paintpot, Fountain Paintpot and the Grand Prismatic Spring.

Yellowstone is one of the world's most famous volcanic landscapes, with thousands of manifestations of the activity taking place 3 miles (5 km) beneath the surface. Steam gasps out of the rocks at vents known as fumaroles. In mud pools, rich suspensions of silt bubble and gurgle like boiling chocolate. At Minerva Terrace, hot springs have created a wedding cake of tiered calcite basins, each dripping with icicle-like stalactites. Most famous of all are the geysers: the Midway Geyser Basin contains 12 of them, firing off at their own idiosyncratic intervals.

This is a fascinating landscape in summer, drawing several million visitors every year. In the dead of the six-month winter, when the tourists have retreated along with the herds of elk, it is perhaps even more extraordinary. The hot springs shroud the valleys in dense blankets of swirling mist. Fluffy balls of snow sit perched on rocks like giant marshmallows, where the surrounding earth, heated from below, has melted the rest of the snow cover.

COLOUR SPLASH *The warm mineral-rich waters of a geyser-fed lake at Yellowstone encourage bacteria and algae to form mats of vivid colour.*

LIVING WITH HOT SPRINGS

The Maoris in and around Rotorua have long appreciated the benefits of geothermal energy. In Whakarewarewa, a traditional village on the edge of the city, Maoris still use the hot springs for bathing, and they cook food by placing pots in flax baskets and lowering them into hot pools. Modern technology has also been used to harness this natural energy. Many homes and buildings in Rotorua are heated in winter with steam drawn from the springs, and refrigeration units are powered from the same source in the summer. To the south, at Wairakei, a geothermal power station produces electricity from bores drilled to access underground supplies of steam.

Mosses and flowers grow here throughout the year, as if enjoying a perpetual summer. In the remote South Sandwich Islands in the South Atlantic, the only plants on the ice-bound volcanic slopes of Bellinghausen are the mosses and liverworts that grow on the warm ground around the steam vents.

LAND OF ICE AND FIRE

Volcanic activity is a part of life in Iceland. Most of the buildings in the capital Reykjavik are heated by water piped from thermal springs. Numerous glasshouses produce tropical flowers and early crops of vegetables, even bananas, from the warmth generated by volcanic heat. Reykjavik's name refers to volcanic activity: it means 'smoking bay'.

There are about 100 active volcanoes in Iceland, and hundreds of other thermal sites. One of the most famous is the volcanically powered waterspout called Geysir at Haukadalur, where superheated water is blasted 300 ft (90 m) into the sky every 90 minutes or so. This so fascinated scientists in the 19th century that its name was applied to all similar phenomena in the world: geysers. The Icelandic name simply means 'gusher'. The Strokkur geyser nearby is almost as famous: it erupts every two minutes.

Iceland is also a place of icefields and glaciers. The largest glacier is Vatnajökull, covering 3300 sq miles (8550 km^2). Underneath it are volcanoes and hot springs, which carve out caves and tunnels in the ice and turn parts of its surface into pools, lakes and rivers. About once a decade heightened volcanic activity turns a large part of the glacier into a sea of slush and broken ice, and if the restraining barrier of lower ice is breached, a torrent called a *jökullaup* suddenly hurtles down the valley at speeds of up to 60 mph (95 km/h), causing widespread damage.

EARTHLY POWERS *A power station in Iceland harnesses the energy of magma-heated water.*

Some animal larvae, snails and water beetles live in the springs themselves, surviving high temperatures. Water beetles and roundworms can tolerate temperatures of up to 45°C (113°F). Some mosquito larvae grow in water so hot and alkaline that it scorches human skin. Bacteria thrive in hot springs. Visitors tempted to take a plunge into warm lakes such as those around Rotorua in New Zealand are advised not to put their heads under water – it contains bacteria notorious for causing earache. Bacteria can survive even higher temperatures. Following the eruption of Mount St Helens in Washington state, USA, some of the hot pools were found to contain the bacteria legionella, responsible for

GURGLE, PLOP! *Geothermal activity keeps the cream-like contents of boiling mudpots at Bumpass Hell in California constantly on the bubble.*

causing the lethal Legionnaire's disease. Even debris from the eruption at an estimated temperature of 600°C (1100°F) had failed to sterilise the area.

THE ORIGIN OF LIFE?

Places like these are where life may well have begun. Some 3500 million years ago, the Earth was beginning to calm down after a billion years of combustion. Rain poured down on a world convulsed by volcanic activity and electrical storms, and the warm pools and shallows filled with rich broths of chemical compounds. Some of these, notably carbon compounds and amino acids, joined up to form clusters and long chains. Somehow – and no one knows how – a vital bridge was crossed when a compound appeared that was capable of replicating itself: deoxyribonucleic acid (DNA). From this, living cells began to develop – early forms of bacteria, the simplest forms of life. Later, about 2000 million years ago, they began to manufacture organic material by the process of photosynthesis using the energy of the sun, with the help of the green pigment chlorophyll.

These organisms are called blue-greens or cyanophytes. Slightly more complex than simple bacteria, they combined in shallow water to form strings of filaments or mats – the 'primordial slime'. In time, some created communities several miles deep. For photosynthesis the blue-greens absorbed hydrogen from water, and thereby released the oxygen molecules that combine with hydrogen to form water. The work of billions of these organisms

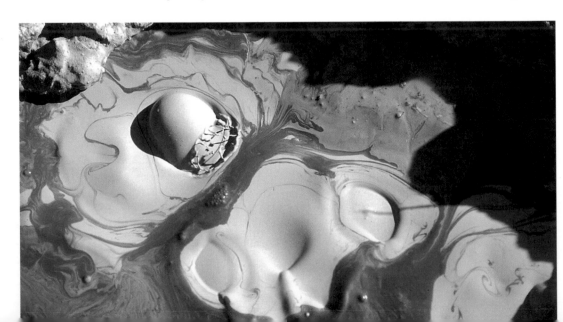

over several hundred million years created the oxygen on which all other living organisms depend. About 1200 million years ago, more complex organisms were formed from combinations of cells, though it took another 200 million years before sponge-like creatures emerged as the first kinds of larger, independently feeding animals.

The history of primordial slime is recorded in rocks, some dating back to 3500 million years ago, others to 500 million years ago, when the slime began to recede. Fossil mats of blue-greens have been found near the Great Lakes of Canada. Similar mats of living growth have been found in shallow seas off Western Australia and the Bahamas. They

FROM THE PAST *Stromatolytes in the waters of Hamelin Pool, Western Australia, are rare modern survivors of some of the earliest life forms on Earth.*

have survived in isolated places where currents are strong or the water is highly saline – conditions avoided by their predators, such as molluscs, which feed off their slime. These strange, rigid clumps are called stromatolites, which means 'stony carpet'. Shapeless and unimportant though they might appear, they may well hold the key to the origins of life on Earth.

PRIMORDIAL SLIME *Blue-green algae grow abundantly in the hot waters of the Warbrick Terraces in New Zealand's Waimangu thermal reserve.*

STILL WATERS

All lakes bear the stamp of their own individuality, moulded by their particular setting, the hue of their water, the mood of the climate and their unique ecology. Many exude such a strong 'spirit of place' that they are considered sacred.

Gold prospectors first came to the mountains and forests of the Cascade Range of Oregon in the north-western USA in the 1850s – but it was many years before they became aware of Crater Lake. It is a wonder that such a vast natural feature remained hidden from them so long, but they had other things on their minds. The local Indians, the Klamath, made no mention of it. To them it was sacred, the one-time abode of the Llao, lord of the underworld, and the site of a great cosmic battle. Their medicine men visited the lake to renew their powers; young warriors swam in it to test their courage. It was a place of spiritual power – and not for the eyes of intruders.

When a group of army hunters stumbled upon the lake in 1865, during a prolonged war with the Klamaths, an astounding sight greeted their eyes. Settled in a huge caldera some 6 miles (10 km) across and about 2000 ft (600 m) below the rim of jagged lava cliffs and scree was a sheet of water of intense ultramarine blueness. One of the party expressed their wonder, declaring: 'That's the sky we're looking at. How have we got so far above it?'

JEWEL IN THE CROWN *The brilliant blue of Crater Lake in Oregon is a product of its immense depth and the purity of the water.*

BLUE WATERS IN SIBERIA: LAKE BAIKAL

This is by far the deepest lake in the world, and by far the largest – by volume. Plunging to depths of 6365 ft (940 m), and occupying a yawning, banana-shaped rift along a fault line in southern Siberia, it is estimated to contain more water than all the Great Lakes of North America put together, and one-fifth of all the fresh water in the world. The deep-blue water is so pure, especially in spring, that it is possible to see objects on the lake floor to a depth of nearly 130 ft (40 m). In winter a thick layer of ice – so thick that trucks can be driven over the lake – may be as clear as a sheet of glass, and fish can be seen swimming below it.

But the lake is a place of changing moods, often shrouded in dense fog or whipped into a fearsome frenzy by winds whipping off the Mongolian steppes. Because of the volume of water in the lake, ice forms and melts slowly, and is present from November to June.

More than three-quarters of the wildlife in the lake is unique to it,

ICY WATERS *Slow to cool and slow to warm, Lake Baikal freezes over late, in December, but ice is still present in June.*

perhaps explained by the lake's extremely ancient origins, 23 million years ago. Creatures include various kinds of freshwater sponge and numerous species of shrimps; the transparent, scaleless golomyanka fish that spends the days at 5250 ft (1600 m) and the nights at the surface; outsized and vividly coloured flatworms; and the silvery Baikal nerpa, the world's only

freshwater seal. No one is quite sure how the first nerpas got here: they are closely related to the ringed seal of the Arctic Ocean, but that is half a continent away. It is possible that they made their way upriver when the distances were shorter – during the last Ice Age over 12 000 years ago.

FRESHWATER SEAL *Baikal nerpas are found mainly around the Uskani Islands in the middle of the lake.*

Later investigations showed that the lake plunges to a depth of 1932 ft (589 m). The extraordinary blueness of the water is a result of this depth. As with most other deep lakes, the other colours of the spectrum are absorbed one by one at different levels – red at about 25 ft (8 m) deep, orange at 150 ft (46 m), yellow at 300 ft (90 m), green at 350 ft (110 m) – leaving in the end only blue.

The lake fills a void created when the volcanic innards of Mount Mazama collapsed about 7000 years ago. Since then rain and heavy snow – which fall from September to May – have gradually filled the caldera to reach an equilibrium whereby annual precipitation matches evaporation and seepage. No river leads out of the lake.

The water is remarkably pure – so pure that turquoise-green aquatic moss can grow at a record depth of 425 ft (130 m). It hosts its own limited assortment of water life. Bacteria live around volcanic vents in the depths, and crayfish inhabit the steeply inclined drop-offs. How they got here remains a mystery, as the lake is isolated from any other water source: perhaps they were dropped by one of the ospreys or black cormorants that visit the crater from time to time.

Apart from the occasional lump of floating pumice, only two islands break the disc of blue. One is an ancient remnant of volcanic activity predating the present caldera, a curiously shaped cluster of rock called the Phantom Ship. The other, called Wizard Island, is a near-perfect cone of black lava that,

about 4000 years ago, was pushed up from the base of the present caldera to a height of 763 ft (232 m) above the lake waters.

Even without the accumulations of Indian legend, this is an awe-inspiring place, which leaves visitors in a state of hushed wonder. Looking out from the crater rim onto the plains below, it seems all the more extraordinary, for this – the deepest freshwater lake in the USA – lies at a height of some 6000 ft (1830 m) above sea level, a vast body of water surrounded by sky.

SACRED BEAUTY

The still beauty of lakes seems to touch the human soul more readily than just about any other kind of scenery. For Russians, Lake Baikal in southern Siberia has a place in their hearts similar to that of the Grand Canyon for Americans. It is more than just a national monument: it is a place that symbolises the scale and grandeur of Russia itself. Thousands dream of visiting Lake Baikal, ideally on their honeymoons. This explains the outcry when the Soviet government built a cellulose factory close to its southern extremity, where the River Angara begins its long journey to the Arctic Ocean. Although the damage has been limited, any blemish on the purity of this lake is deeply resented. To the Buryats, a Mongol people who have lived in the Baikal region since long before the first Russian fur trappers

SACRED LAKE *Prayer flags left by Buddhist pilgrims to Lake Manasarovar are said to recite sacred mantras as they flutter in the wind.*

and gold prospectors arrived in the mid-17th century, the lake represents even more. For them, it is holy and the lake island of Olkhon the abode of a powerful god where shamanistic rituals are still performed.

This feeling for their lake is nothing unique; other peoples and religions revere other lakes in similar ways. One of the most sacred places for Hindus and Buddhists, for example, is Lake Manasarovar, a stunningly beautiful stretch of pure water that lies at 15 052 ft (4588 m) above sea level in southwestern Tibet, surrounded by desolate mountains on the roof of the world. It is said to have been created in the mind of the god Brahma, and is believed to be the abode of Shiva, god of destruction and reproduction, in his incarnation as a swan. It forms part of the great pilgrimage route to nearby Mount Kailas. Devotees walk around the lake and bathe in it, and they collect the

water in bottles as holy relics. It was here that the ashes of the great Indian leader Mahatma Gandhi were finally scattered after his death in 1948.

SAPPHIRE BLUE AND TURQUOISE

Many lakes are celebrated for their extraordinary colour – or colours – a result of their mineral content as well as depth. A series of 16 lakes drops through the karst (limestone) landscape of Plitvice, on the border between Croatia and Bosnia, linked by a necklace of waterfalls and foaming rivulets. In winter it turns into a magical landscape of frozen movement, with huge icicles clinging to the lips of waterfalls. In spring the streams and rivers gush and roar as they strive to channel the torrents of meltwater pouring down from the surrounding hills. Then, as the calm of summer descends upon the neighbouring woodlands, the lakes unveil

SKY BLUE *In the clear, thin air of the Hindu Kush, the Band-e Amir lakes glow with an unreal intensity enhanced by the presence of algae in the water.*

their extraordinary colours – ranging from a deep blue to a stunning turquoise.

Here, the water is given its colour by the calcium carbonate in the limestone of the surrounding karst landscape. As the mineral content of the water changes, so do the lakes' colours. Other things change, too. Fallen tree trunks in the lake beds quickly turn a ghostly white as they are encrusted with precipitated lime. The waterways are constantly altering as the lime, sometimes incorporating moss or algae, builds new rims around the different lakes and on the cusps of falls.

Some lakes take on the colour of the various sediments that flow into them. Lake Turkana (formerly Lake Rudolf) in the Great Rift Valley in northern Kenya is stained a reddish-orange hue from volcanic deposits

and the heavy silt tipped into it by the River Omo which, somewhat bizarrely, flows across the lake in its own aqueduct lined with deposited silt. The lake contains a large number of Nile perch which feed a population of crocodiles and birds such as ibises and spoonbills, as well as the families of fishermen who fish by night using dome-shaped baskets.

No one is sure what produces the colours of the lakes of Keli Muti on the island of Flores in Indonesia. Three lakes sit in the craters of adjacent volcanoes, each a different colour – deep brown, green and pale green. The colours may be caused by the mineral content of the water – but they have been known to change. During the 1960s they were various shades of brown and blue. Algae in the water may also be responsible. This is certainly the case with the Band-e Amir lakes high in the Hindu Kush of Afghanistan, whose shades

CLOSE TO NATURE *The Plitvice lakes, in one of Croatia's prized national parks, have wooden pontoons and walkways to link the woodland paths.*

of stunning blue and green are created by a mixture of depth, light effects and algae.

Algae are found suspended in almost all bodies of water. They live on nutrients such as nitrogen and phosphorus; the richer the nutrients and the warmer the water, the

more robust they grow – so lakes are often clearer in spring than in summer. Rapid growth in algae, or 'blooms', may turn a lake green, and even result in a choking layer of blue-green or even reddish-brown scum. Algae form the vital first link in the food chain of lakes. They are food for numerous small creatures, such as animate plankton, protozoans and crustaceans, as well as many larger ones.

A WORLD IN A LAKE

All lakes – even the mighty Baikal – are microcosms, each a unique coming together of the life that has converged on it over time. This effect can be seen in miniature in the ponds called *tinajas* (a Spanish word for a large water jar) in the arid south-west of North America and in the Chichuahan Desert of northern Mexico. Isolated among the rocks of remote canyons, they provide vital water holes for mule deer and pronghorns – but also contain their own worlds of competing and interacting life, including frogs, snakes and aquatic insects.

The Chichuahan Desert has another series of remote lakes, set among gypsum dunes, which have such clear water that they have been called 'natural aquariums'. In the Cuatro Ciénegas ('Four Marshes') there are tetra and cichlid fish, shrimps and aquatic snails, as well as other rare fish and some reptiles such as the coahuilan pupfish and box turtle.

Lake animals may be specialists in the first place, or they may become specialists through the dictates of their habitat. Nowhere is this better seen than in and around salt lakes, where the evaporation of trapped water has

led to ever-increasing concentrations of the residue minerals. Fresh water contains one-seventh of the minerals of seawater; it accounts for no more than 3 per cent of the water on Earth, yet it, rather than seawater, sustains virtually all living things on land. Salt lakes have an even richer concentration of minerals than the sea, containing up to six times more of them. Living in such a habitat requires particular specialisation and powers of adaptation.

Australia has one of the world's most spectacular salt lakes, albeit an intermittent one. Until the 1840s, the European settlers around the rim of the continent had no idea what lay in its centre. Some speculated that it might be a great inland sea. Once every eight years, on average, they were almost right. After very heavy rains, water rushes down the western flanks of the Great

DISAPPEARING ACT *Clumps of salt in Lake Eyre – witness to centuries of repeated flooding and evaporation. More often than not, the lake is dry.*

MEETING POINT *Waterholes dot the salt-encrusted Etosha Pan providing sustenance for the herds that migrate across the region in the dry season.*

RED SHIFT *The blue-green algae and other organisms that thrive in Lake Natron sometimes smother the surface with a mat of red sludge, pierced only by hot springs.*

Dividing Range and heads across the desert along the paths of dry riverbeds. Usually it dries up in the riverbeds, but occasionally enough water accumulates to create a large lake at the lowest point – a depression in central southern Australia called Lake Eyre. It is only a lake for as long as it takes the sun to evaporate the water – from a few months to two years – after which all that remains is a flat, rippled surface encrusted with the mineral salts left behind by some 12 000 years of evaporation since the lake was permanently full during the last glacial period.

During the months when the lake is filled with water, the region is dramatically transformed. Shrimps that survived in the soil as dormant eggs suddenly spring into life, joining tadpoles and fish that have been swept into the lake with the floodwater. These attract birds such as cormorants, gulls and ducks. Breeding pelicans arrive and take up residence on the

shore, which is now strewn with wildflowers that have popped up from dormant seeds.

As the lake dries up in temperatures of 38°C (100°F) or more, all species race to complete their lifeplans – by producing seeds or eggs or mature young. The nesting pelicans fight for diminishing resources as they struggle to rear their young until the young reach an age when they can fend for themselves. They need three months' water supply to achieve this. Usually there is enough water to see this process through, and to ensure that this same pattern of life will return the next time Lake Eyre floods. But sometimes the water dries up too soon, and the shores are littered with the debris and corpses of tragic failures.

Another temporary lake forms over the Etosha Pan in northern Namibia, providing the setting for one of Africa's most impressive cavalcades. In the midst of this dry and hostile world of salt flats – the remnants of a vast ancient lake – are a series of freshwater springs. During the dry season countless animals revive a collective memory of these water holes and head across the pan to their winter pastures to the north-east – wildebeest, zebra, elephants, kudus, giraffes, oryxes, springboks, and accompanying lions,

continued on page 138

UNDERWATER IN AFRICA

Divers accustomed to the glorious, but more familiar, submarine world of a coral reef would be astounded by the extraordinary events that take place beneath the surface of a large African water hole or lake. At the Mzima Springs in the Tsavo National Park in Kenya animals such as elephants, zebras and impalas come to drink at the water's edge. But a quite different world exists, mainly out of sight, in the world at their feet. The most significant animals in the water are the hippos, which spend the day all but submerged, ambling with a slow-motion trot along their underwater paths. They feed on land at night but defecate by day directly into the water. The effect of this is to fertilise the water, recycling the nutrients from the grassy banks for the benefit of a wide variety of bacteria, algae and larvae. These provide the lowest rung of the food chain, which is exploited by frogs and freshwater shrimps; they in turn are eaten by swimming snakes and monitor lizards. Turtles and crocodiles spend their days in and out of the water in search of food, while fish eagles and cormorants dive for gobies and eels, and darters pursue water snakes and other prey. Spotted-necked otters swim in search of fish, but keep a wary eye out for the predatory rock python, 14 ft (4.2 m) long constrictors which lurk in the shallows with only their nostrils protruding.

cheetahs, leopards and hyenas. Then after the beginning of the rains in November, large quantities of water pour onto the plain and create a huge shallow lake surrounded by luxuriant meadows. This is the cue for a mighty migration: thousands of animals now march back across the plains to greet this new pasture, accompanied overhead by flights of flamingos, Egyptian geese, larks and plovers.

The other great salt lakes of Africa are in the east of the continent. A chain of salt and soda lakes stretches south through western Kenya and into Tanzania: Lakes Natron, Magadi (which means soda in Masai), Naivasha, Elementeita, Nakuru and Begoria. Water flows into them, but little flows out, and in the heat of the African sun the minerals – notably soda (sodium carbonate) from the ash of surrounding volcanoes – build up. In some lakes the soda is so condensed that it burns human skin. But several life

LAKES OF PITCH

Some of the world's most peculiar lakes are not full of shimmering water, but are literally pitch black. They are filled with natural asphalt or bitumen, otherwise known as tar or pitch. Natural asphalt, a thickened form of crude oil, appears on the surface in certain places, notably in Trinidad, whose famous Pitch Lake covers an area of 114 acres (46 ha) and is some 200 ft (60 m) deep. The asphalt is exploited for road building, and is so dense around the perimeter that trucks can drive over it. Elsewhere it is viscous enough to be rolled back in sheets, or even fairly liquid. Animals have fallen into the asphalt in the past and the remains

NATURAL TAR *Exposure to the air causes evaporation and hardens the surface pitch – as here on Trinidad's Pitch Lake.*

of a number of prehistoric animals have been found in Pitch Lake.

Even more astonishing are the Rancho La Brea tar pits, in central Los Angeles. These were exploited commercially in the 19th century, but in recent decades the site has become far more famous for the extraordinary quantity of fossils found in them – more than 100 tons of bones in all. These include the remains of giant ground sloths, mammoths and sabre-toothed cats dating from between 40 000 and 10 000 years ago. Most of them must have become entrapped by the sticky tar and probably died of starvation or asphyxiation.

THE COLOUR PINK

From pink to brick-red – flamingos come in a range of shades. None is entirely natural since flamingos take their colour from the food they eat. Their preferred food is algae and microscopic lake organisms. Algae may be green when alive, but they contain other pigments and can turn a deep red when they die. The connection between pigment and food was not appreciated until flamingos were taken to zoos, where they were fed on cereal diets. They lost their colour, which was only regained by including additives, such as carrot oil, in their food.

forms tolerate this, including minuscule protozoans, organisms known as rotifers and algae called spirulina. The algae may be so thick that they collect in slimy mats, especially after a 'bloom'. They provide a rich and plentiful supply of food for the

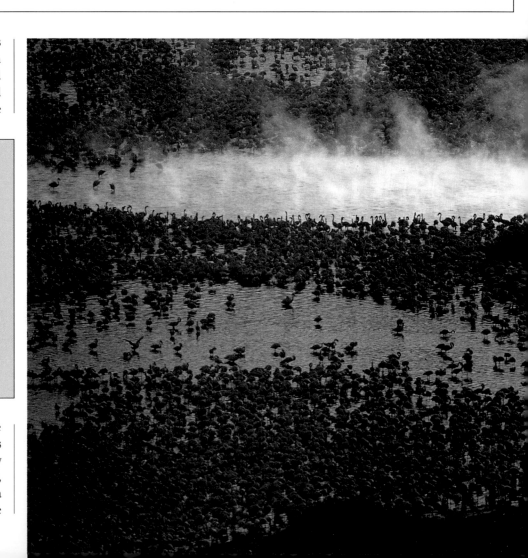

most remarkable inhabitants of these lakes, the flamingos – 3 million lesser flamingos and 50 000 greater flamingos. In their stunning pink and red liveries, they spend their days gathered in throngs, siphoning the algae from the water through their inverted bills. They breed in the relative isolation of the remoter and more inhospitable of the lakes, such as Lake Natron.

Some species of fish can also tolerate these conditions – notably the cichlid *Tilapia grahami* which lives in Lake Magadi, around the hot springs that bubble up in the lake at temperatures of 38°C (100°F). This is one of the fish called 'mouth brooders': the female protects her young by allowing scores

BOUNTIFUL SODA *Flamingos flock to East Africa's soda lakes, such as Lake Bogoria. Hot-water springs create a backdrop of steam.*

of them to shelter inside her mouth. Cichlids form part of the diet of pelicans which breed in and around Lake Elementeita.

Flamingos are also found in the salt lakes that lie in the Altiplano of western Bolivia and south-eastern Peru, some 10 000 ft (3050 m) high in the Andes. They include the rarest of all flamingo species, the deep red James's flamingo. They add to the extraordinary colour of these lakes, tinted by their mineral content. As their names suggest, Laguna Colorado is a deep red and Laguna Verde is emerald green.

North America's best-known salt lake is Lake Mono in California. It is famous for the extraordinary shapes of its pillars of blackened tufa, the unusual result of lime from volcanic springs mixing with the salt in the water. Their shapes have become all the more striking as the level of the lake has dropped by 44 ft (13.5 m) since the 1940s, leaving many previously submerged pillars high and dry.

This drop in water level has been caused by the diversion of water from streams feeding the lake in order to supply Los Angeles with one-sixth of its water needs. It has caused consternation among ecologists, not just because of the threat to the tufa pillars.

BEACHED *Like the wrecks of battleships, tufa blocks in Lake Mono have been exposed by the diversion of water from rivers flowing into the lake.*

Lake Mono is an important landmark on the migration route of Arctic birds and a nesting site for many species, notably grebes and California gulls. Snowy plovers, teal, sandpipers and Wilson's phalarope are all summer visitors, feeding on the lake's rich supplies of brine flies and shrimps. There are no fish.

The most famous of all salt lakes is the Dead Sea, on the borders of Israel and Jordan at the northern end of the Great Rift Valley. At 1299 ft (396 m) below sea level, this is the lowest place on Earth, a cauldron into which, over the last 2 million years, the waters of the Jordan have flowed and then evaporated. It is also the saltiest lake in the world – six times saltier than the average sea. Blocks of congealed salt float in the water, and solid pillar-like salt stacks have accumulated at the shallow southern end. As if to prove the resilience of nature, even in this water there is life – albeit only microscopic single-celled organisms.

LIFE IN THE SHALLOWS

Despite the oceans' immense size and depth, virtually all life in them takes place within 200 ft (60 m) of the surface. This narrow band holds a vast array of fantastically varied and strange life forms, and is one of the richest habitats on Earth.

The world's coasts are battlegrounds, where tides and waves surge relentlessly against the land. Cliffs, sea arches and sea stacks bear witness to the millennia of pounding and scouring that have sculpted the land forms. The meeting point between land and sea is a dynamic interface, and only the toughest insects, crustaceans and other life forms are a match for it.

Rockpools offer oases of calm – but only for a limited time. Crabs, starfish, shrimps, anemones, mussels, marine worms, sea urchins and tiny fish can find brief respite from the waves here, but they all have to be able to cope with the pounding that will inevitably follow when the tide returns. The calm of a rock pool is, in any case, misleading. The inhabitants have been thrown together by chance in an amphitheatre where a reluctant gladiatorial fight will take place, and the losers will be lunch. Shrimps, crabs and fish, dart and hide nervously: any moment of distraction could be their last. The anemones use their delicate tentacles to filter plankton out of the water, stunning the plankton with their stinging cells – also a weapon of defence against sea slugs. Mussels filter for plankton, but might fall victim to a starfish, which can prise a mussel apart by clutching it to its underside and pulling on its shells with its arms; once open the starfish will extrude its stomach into the shell and dissolve the mussel with its digestive juices. To add to the danger, the tide pool could be flooded with rainwater, reducing the salinity to dangerous levels, or it could heat up in the summer sun to intolerable temperatures. These are high-risk environments.

Certain animals move right through the turbulent margins of the coast in order to breed in the relative stability of land. Giant leatherback turtles climb ponderously up their carefully selected beaches in Surinam and Malaysia in order to lay eggs the size of ping-pong balls in holes excavated out of the sand. Most sea snakes likewise come ashore to lay their eggs, as do some of the most extraordinary animals of the sea, horseshoe crabs. These strange, heavily armoured creatures are not crabs at all, but distant relatives of scorpions. They are living fossils, unchanged for 190 million years.

Shallow sea may be a zone of pounding waves, but beneath the surface it is relatively calm. Sunlight illuminates and warms the shallows – and this is where most sea creatures prefer to be – in the first 200 ft (60 m) of the ocean. In tropical and subtropical shallows, conditions may be perfect for the most fruitful of all marine environments: the coral reef.

CORAL SPLENDOURS

Lying off the north-east coast of Australia, stretching for some 1550 miles (2500 km) from north to south, is the the largest coral reef in the world. The Great Barrier Reef is a magnificent string of submerged reefs and low-lying islands, the work of billions of tiny coral polyps over a period of around

PEACEFUL RESPITE *At low tide a tide pool enjoys a few hours of tranquillity, but its residents have to fight their corners in this temporary microcosm.*

10 000 years. It harbours a mesmerising world of spectacular undersea life: home to no fewer than 1500 species of fish, some 4000 species of molluscs and 400 different kinds of corals. The Great Barrier Reef offers a glimpse of a world that existed long before human beings walked the Earth – an ecosystem that has evolved over countless millions of years.

The strange sculptural shapes of the multicoloured coral stands are full of nooks and crannies. They provide an anchor for tube worms, with their fantastic crowns of tentacles, and hiding places for numerous, brilliantly coloured and decorated fish with picturesque names such as butterfly fish, parrotfish, clownfish, painted sweetlips, harlequin tusk fish and fairy basslets. Giant clams, measuring 4 ft (1.2 m) across and weighing 550 lb (250 kg), filter plankton from the water through fleshy bodies spotted with iridescent dots. Anemones, some 3 ft (1 m) across, flutter jewel-like tentacles. Punctiliously spotted cowries burrow in the soft white coral sand. Squid hover,

MAN TRAP? *Giant clams feed by filtering. The idea that divers can be trapped by a giant clam is a myth. They take several minutes to close.*

SIESTA *Brightly hued soft corals close their tentacles when not feeding. Polyps in neighbouring stands of hard coral usually emerge at night to feed.*

pulsing with changing colour, undulating their wings mesmerically before darting off backwards on a jet of water. A green turtle swims by, then a Bedford's flatworm, flapping in the water like a flying carpet. A potato cod, covered with big black spots, moves with a ponderous, jerky rhythm, keeping a wary eye on a white-tipped reef shark.

Here and there, huge moray eels – some as attractively mottled as any sea creature –

peer out mistrustfully from their lairs, all ready and waiting to snatch a passing fish. Although fearsome-looking, some morays, accustomed to divers, will even eat fish from their hands. In a similar fashion, stingrays of

'Stingray City' in the sandy shallows off the coast of the island of Grand Cayman at times drop their fearsome guise and allow themselves to be stroked.

HIDE AND SEEK

Such tameness is misleading. Generally this multicoloured, bejewelled world is also an extremely ruthless one. As morays dart out from their hiding places, sharks and shoals of barracuda or tuna sweep through the reefs on the hunt for food. Most fish living in coral reefs have evolved defence mechanisms to ensure their survival against this constant threat. The trunkfish is protected by a bony, box-like skeleton; pufferfish can blow themselves up into spine-covered footballs; surgeonfish have scalpel-sharp spines on either side of their tail. Triggerfish are so called because they are able to raise a rigid trigger-shaped dorsal spine and wedge themselves into crevices, from which no predator can extract them.

At night, when many of the corals, the tube worms and the sea fans come into full flower, the reef becomes transformed into an Aladdin's cave of glowing and bejewelled luminescence. But this is also the time when many predators, notably the sharks,

are at their most active. The parrotfish for one goes into hiding. Settling into the shelter of a handy crevice, it envelops itself in a bubble of mucus, which conceals its scent while it rests.

Camouflage is a vital form of defence on the coral reef, and many creatures have evolved ingenious solutions. Butterfly fish have a large eye-shaped dot on their upper rear quarter – confusing predators that might expect them to dart in the opposite direction. Long, thin trumpet fish flip themselves so that they float vertically rather than horizontally, hovering motionless next to strands of weed. There is even a species of shark, the wobbegong, that finds it advantageous to resort to disguise: the wobbegong looks like a shaggy carpet of seaweed and can rest unobtrusively on the sea floor. Scorpionfish and stonefish look like shapeless algae-covered rocks, and they have another defence as well.

GENTLE COUSINS *Camouflage allows wobbegong, members of the shark family, to live unobtrusively on the seabed – but they bite if stepped upon.*

The spines on their backs are armed with a poison that delivers a lethal sting to anything that touches it. Stonefish have a powerful toxin that affects muscles, which can induce death by preventing a victim from breathing or by causing cardiac arrest.

Among the most fantastically shaped and coloured creatures of the coral reef are the sea slugs or nudibranches ('naked gill') – some of which grow to 1 ft (30 cm) in length. With their exuberant tassels and flamboyant colours, they demonstrate the

SUBMARINE INFLATABLE *When threatened, pufferfish can quickly inflate their bodies with water and air to form a ball of spines twice their normal size.*

NIGHTLIGHTS IN THE SEA

Dive into the sea on a dark Caribbean night and your body will create an explosive trail of magical beads of lights. The cause is thousands of tiny plankton called dinoflagellates which are excited by movement to produce a remarkable volume of light. No one knows why they do this: it cannot help them in their fight for survival on the lowest rung of the food chain. But they offer a service to other animals by sending out a shower of alarm signals at every movement of a large predator.

Numerous marine animals exhibit the phenomenon called

'bioluminescence' – the ability to emit light through biological processes. Some 1000 species of fish have this ability. One of the most remarkable is the *Photoblepharon* or 'flashlight fish' found in the Red Sea and parts of the Indian and Pacific oceans. Shoals create shimmering clouds of bluish-green light on dark nights. Flashlight fish have large light-emitting organs beneath their eyes, which they can

ILLUMINATIONS *The natural, pulsating grace of cuttlefish is enhanced at night by rows of bioluminescent spots.*

flash on and off with a flap of skin. The light comes from cultures containing millions of light-generating bacteria. The fish may use their light to attract prey, such as plankton and crustaceans: the lights are sited conveniently close to both their eyes and their mouth. They also appear to use their lights to send signals, as a means of locating each other, and in mating rituals. If alarmed they swim off in a zigzag pattern, flashing in quick succession – an effective way of confusing predators. Since the lights continue to glow even after the fish has died, fishermen catch flashlight fish and use the cheeks as bait for night fishing.

A number of the group of marine invertebrates known as echinoderms, such as starfish, sea urchins, sea cucumbers and brittlestars, also glow at night. These glows may be defence mechanisms, designed to frighten off predators, such as crabs. Squid are well known for releasing

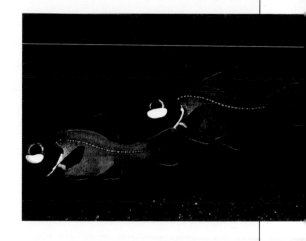

EYE FLASH *The flashing light emitted by flashlight fish comes from patches of bacteria located just beneath the eyes.*

clouds of ink to confuse an enemy: some go a step further and spray a cloud of light. Many squid, jellyfish, comb jellies, sea slugs and marine worms are also equipped with nightlights, often dispersed decoratively along the seam-like lines that divide their bodies.

Some krill emit such prodigious quantities of light that researchers have been able to read at night using jars containing just half a dozen of them.

KNOW YOUR ENEMY *The spines that line the back of stonefish are capable of delivering a debilitating, if not fatal, shot of poison.*

extraordinary variety and ingenuity of design found among so many marine creatures. These sea slugs eat anemones: they are immune to their poison, and store it in concentrated form in the frond-like gills on their backs, providing them with a kind of secondhand defence system. Their colour serves as a warning signal to predators.

The poison in many undersea creatures is particularly virulent, mainly because fish are comparatively immune to venom. The bite of the yellow-banded sea snake is more venomous than the bite of any other snake

SEA HARLEQUINS *Sea slugs'
bright colours are a measure
of their confidence. Eaters of
other poisonous sea creatures,
they themselves are often toxic.*

in the world. One of the most dangerous
creatures of Australian waters is a cone
shell, which delivers highly toxic poison on
a dart shot out of a long tube.

DEADLY JELLIES

Jellyfish can also deliver painful stings –
which can sometimes be fatal. The box
jellyfish of the Great Barrier Reef is the
most virulent, and has been responsible for

HANDS TO READ BY

Many of the shallow waters off Japan are
inhabited by *Cypridina hilgendorfii*, tiny
crustaceans also known as 'sea fireflies'
because they glow at night. It was discovered
that the chemicals responsible for this luminescence function after sea fireflies are not
only dead, but dried. In the Second World
War the Japanese dried them in huge quantities. They were ground into powder and
dispatched to soldiers in the field. The users
added water and rubbed the mixture on their
fingers, and there was nature's own torch –
ideal for reading maps and orders by night.

---

killing more people this century than
sharks. By comparison, the notorious Portuguese man-of-war is tame. Despite its
reputation, the sting of a Portuguese man-
of-war is rarely fatal, although extremely
painful. Its tentacles, which can be up to
33 ft (10 m) long, spread from the gas-filled
sac that drifts on the surface at the mercy of
the winds.

In fact, the Portuguese man-of-war is
not a jellyfish, but a siphonophore – in other

words, a cooperative colony of
four different kinds of polyps,
each with a different function.
As with jellyfish, the tentacles
disable the prey; then they
winch it up to the body where it
is fed into the digestive cavity.
One fish, however, is immune to the sting:
the nomeid Portuguese man-of-war fish
lives happily among the tentacles, feeding
off scraps from its host's meals. Another immune creature is a species of nudibranch
that feeds off Portuguese men-of-war. It
floats on the surface of the sea on a packet
of bubbles in order to find its prey – and it
uses the toxins in its prey to arm its own for-
midable sting.

Jellyfish are primitive creatures, but they
are capable of movement, the rhythmic pul-
sations of their transparent
bodies making them some of
the most beautiful of all undersea creatures. In the islands of
Palau in the western Pacific,
they use their movement in an
unusual way. The islands include a collection of shallow
inlets fed by the sea. Some of
these are more like sea lakes,
accessed only by narrow tunnels. One such inlet is the
home of millions of jellyfish
which have grown too big to
pass out of the exit. These jellyfish do not sting, because they
do not feed on prey. Instead,
they contain algae which manufacture food for them. To do
this, however, they need sunlight – consequently, this vast

DEADLY JELLY *The box
jellyfish's venom-packed
tentacles grow to 10 ft (3 m)
long and deliver a sting that
can cause death in five minutes.*

mass of jellyfish, sometimes as much as 20 ft
(6 m) deep, moves about the inlet as the
day progresses, following the sun. As it does
so the jellyfish in it rotate, in order to bathe
the algae in equal amounts of light. At
night they gravitate towards the bottom of
the inlet, where they absorb nutrient-rich
supplies of ammonia.

SERVICES RENDERED

Cooperative behaviour among different
species is often explained as a means of
protection against predators. Shoals of fish,
for example, find safety in numbers and
can disconcert attacking predators by darting out in all directions. But the undersea
world is not all about aggression: it also
involves an extraordinary and complex
network of cooperation and mutually beneficial behaviour among species.

Some types of clownfish are covered by
a secretion that makes them immune to the
stings of anemones. They live safely among
the tentacles of an anemone, protected by
its poison, and in return may help to keep

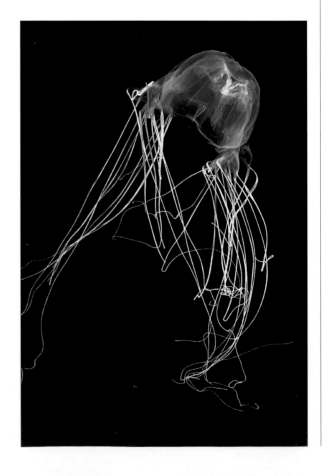

THE MAGIC OF CORAL

It is one of the wonders of nature that the Great Barrier Reef, the largest structure on Earth created by a living thing, has been built by an animal as tiny, delicate and fragile as a coral polyp. Polyps are related to jellyfish and sea anemones. They feed by siphoning plankton through their tentacles, usually at night, when they emerge from their hard limestone homes and create a velvety landscape of brilliant colours. Dead coral is white, but living coral is green, pink, yellow, violet, brown – in fact, just about any colour from an artist's palette. As coral polyps feed, they extract minerals from the sea to secrete the lime that forms their hard outer skeletons. A stand of branching coral such as *Acropora* may grow 12 in (30 cm) in a year on a reef's seaward side where the nutrients are more plentiful; other more solidly shaped corals increase by just 1/8 in (3 mm) a year. Some larger colonies, called 'bommies' in Australia, are 1200 years old.

These reef-building corals grow only in the warmer waters of the world, in a band that extends its limits slightly wider than those of the tropics. The warm, salty water must be deep enough to cover them, but shallow enough to ensure that they receive plenty of sunlight. Reef-building coral will not grow at depths greater than 165 ft (50 m). They need the sunlight because they are not alone in their endeavours: coral polyps may create coral reefs, but they work in tandem with tiny marine algae, zooxanthellae, which live within them, using the energy from the sun to manufacture nutrients and oxygen for the polyps. Coral reefs, therefore, are effectively animal, mineral and vegetable.

Polyps are capable of producing both male and female reproductive cells. On spring nights they create underwater blizzards by releasing billions of packets of eggs and sperm into the water. The eggs that are fertilised produce larvae, which may eventually attach themselves to a suitable base and begin a new colony. The colony multiplies as the founding polyp replicates itself by producing new buds.

There are about 700 species of reef-building coral in the world,

SOFT TOUCH *Soft corals take a variety of guises. This giant soft leather coral is found in the Red Sea and southern Pacific.*

each with its own shape, colour and reef structure. In the seas at the frontier between the Pacific and the Indian oceans, a single coral reef may contain 400 different species of coral. Elkhorn, finger, flower, cactus, mushroom, brain, table, plate, lettuce – all such coral names represent an attempt to categorise the fantastic range of shapes which the corals create.

But some corals do not create reefs at all: the so-called soft corals do not contain algae, and so can live at greater depths, and they are found through most of the world's oceans, and even polar seas. They grow on flexible skeletons that bend to the currents and flow of the sea. Although not hard they form impressive structures, such as the so-called gorgonian sea fans.

DENSE BRAIN *A solid lump of brain coral sits in a colourful nest of purple polyps.*

TRANSPARENT PERFECTION

Plankton have been called the 'grass of the oceans'. These tiny life forms represent the bottom line of the sea's food chain, and all sea creatures ultimately depend on them. Many marine creatures, such as sponges and coral polyps, live by feeding directly off the plankton. By a strange paradox, the oceans' largest creatures, the blue whales, whale sharks, basking sharks and manta rays, are also plankton eaters.

The term plankton covers a range of life forms. Their name comes from the Greek *planktos*, 'wandering'. Some are plants, some animals; some forms – such as dinoflagellates – fall in between. The plants, such as the single-celled algae called diatoms, are called phytoplankton (from the Greek *phuton*, meaning 'a plant'). Animal forms – which cannot photosynthesise and so must consume plankton that do – are called zooplankton. These in turn are divided into two groups. Some, such as the shrimp-like copepods,

OCEAN GEMS *Plankton, such as these diatoms and mollusc larvae, reveal a mesmerising array of colours and shapes.*

will never be anything but plankton and are termed 'permanent'. Others are 'temporary': the tiny larval forms of marine creatures such as crabs, sponges, sea urchins, starfish and coral polyps. If they are not eaten, they will develop into the adult form of their species.

Most plankton are about the size of a pinhead. But they have an importance out of all proportion to their size. One of the by-products of photosynthesis is the oxygen we breathe. Sea plants – and phytoplankton in particular – are believed to be responsible for 70 per cent of the world's oxygen.

damaged by a plague of crown-of-thorns starfish, which moved across the coral heads eating the polyps. It looked for a time as if this plague might destroy the entire system. The onslaught has been controlled. Human intervention was important as was another creature of the reef, the giant triton snail, which attacks crown-of-thorns starfish, overcoming their poisonous spines.

A rise in the sea temperature can also make coral reefs die. When the temperature rose a few degrees off Tahiti recently, corals expelled their algae partners causing 'bleaching' – which can lead to coral death. Corals need clean, clear water, and pollution poses a threat. Off the Florida coast, coral is dying from the choking effect of excess algae, which have developed because of increased nutrients such as phosphorus and nitrogen in the water, probably related to the emission of fertiliser residue from the Mississippi Delta and the reclaimed Everglades.

RED SEA WONDERS

The Red Sea is famous among divers for having some of the best collections of coral reefs and the richest underwater life in the world – and one of the greatest threats here

it free of parasites. Another example of such cooperation involves one type of goby which shares a hole with a shrimp. The shrimp digs the hole, and the goby hunts and provides scraps of food for the shrimp – and both share the refuge of the hole.

Sometimes queues of large fish can be seen lining up near a particular clump of coral. At the head of the queue a group of small black-and-yellow fish busy themselves around the first fish in the line. They are cleaner wrasse, and they live by cleaning bacteria and debris from the skin, the gills and even the mouths of other fish. Bigger fish appear to know that this is a vital service. They patiently wait their turn at the 'cleaning station'; then they remain quite still and benign while the wrasse perform their task. To show that they are ready, and to make it clear that only cleaning is being offered, not a meal, the wrasse first of all do a kind of shimmying dance. Size is no object to them: they will clean huge manta rays – even scuba divers. This is not the only

example of undersea cleaning services: in temperate waters cleaner shrimps will use their delicate arms to pick parasites off the skin of moray eels.

THREATS TO CORAL

Everything beneath the sea is in a state of flux, constantly adjusting the complex formulae of checks and balances. Coral reefs themselves grow and decline. Corals are sensitive creatures, and have many enemies. Parrotfish eat polyps by scrunching up corals with their beak-like mouths; golden horn snails also feed on corals. During the 1980s about a third of the Great Barrier Reef was

LETHAL BEAUTY *The jewel-like beauty of sea anemones belies their ability to deliver a powerful, stunning sting through their tentacles.*

is posed by the hundreds of thousands of divers who visit it each year.

Around the reefs there are the usual assortments of brilliantly coloured fish such as emperor angelfish, butterfly fish and Picasso triggerfish. Other more unusual inhabitants include a species of angler fish which disguises itself as a spongy gargoyle and remains stock still in its crevice dangling a bait-like organ from a spine in front of its open mouth. If an unsuspecting fish is attracted to the bait the angler darts forward and swallows it.

Bordered by desert and parched mountains, the coral reefs of the Red Sea are like a miraculous oasis of life. But the desert also has an impact on the sea. Over thousands of years water from the desert wadis (normally dry watercourses that fill after rain) has poured into the sea, carrying tons of sand with it. Coral cannot survive in water clouded by sand. Instead, flat expanses of sand have spread out over the sea floor – an underwater desert.

Because there are few places to hide here, fish have adopted cunning strategies of survival. Sand-coloured stargazer fish – so-called because of the upward-looking, bulbous eyes on the top of their heads – lie in perfect camouflage on the seabed. All that is visible is a zipper-like mouth, at the ready to snap up passing prey, which the fish appears to detect by sensing movement through an electrical field. Flounders, speckled like the sand, can stop still on the sea floor and, in a flash, ruffle up the sand to merge completely with it.

The spectacular lionfish, as decorous as a Chinese festival lion with its stripes and fan-like fins, has no need for camouflage. Like its relative the stonefish, it carries a highly toxic poison in its spines, and its coloration and demeanour give sufficient warning of this to predators. Sea urchins, filtering plankton on the sandy floor, are similarly well protected by their long spines, while hermit crabs live in the protection of their borrowed shells. They need to change their shells as they grow. Usually they locate abandoned shells, and quickly transfer their soft bodies into them. Occasionally, in desperation, they will forcibly remove the legitimate tenant of a shell that they covet – and will even adopt tin cans and coconut shells.

Colonies of specialist eels have taken over parts of this desert sea. They dig long thin holes in the sand, which they line with mucus. Then they spend their lives in the

RED SEA KALEIDOSCOPE *With a vast range of corals, fish and other sea creatures, the Red Sea offers a showcase for the multifaceted riches of the submarine world.*

NEEDLE SHARP *Red urchins off the coast of British Columbia are armed with long spines. Despite this, they have enemies, such as wolf eels, that brave the spines to reach the flesh inside.*

array. Weaverfish – like stonefish but less dangerous – lie buried in the sand with spines protruding from them. Some species of crabs take on fantastic disguises. Sponge crabs allow large wads of sponge to grow on their shells, while the so-called decorator crabs plant their shells with flowing strands of seaweed, coloured according to the background they choose to live in.

In the Strait of Georgia, between Vancouver Island and mainland Canada, the sea floor is adorned with red sea urchins, white mushroom-like anemones 2 ft (60 cm) tall, fancifully decorated nudibranches, feathery sea pens and sea stars, relatives of starfish but with a dozen or more arms.

Vertical piles, such as those used to support piers are often crammed with sea life. Mussels, oysters, barnacles and limpets grip the wood in clusters, creating a surface over which crabs can scurry. Bobbly sea squirts and algae such as sea lettuce also find anchorage on the wood, while small fish such as blennies and perhaps seahorses hover around looking for scraps and plankton.

Even the bitterly cold waters of polar regions are teeming with life. Beneath 6 ft (1.8 m) of Antarctic ice are strange red spider crabs, starfish and their wispy cousins crinoids, luminescent jellyfish and multicoloured sponges. Where freezing brine drips through from the surface, spires of ice are sometimes formed, like underwater stalactites or pillars; and sometimes the sea freezes to the seabed, pinning the animals to the ground. After a thaw the blocks of ice float to the surface with starfish, sponges and fish still

hole, poking the upper part of their body out to catch any particles of food floating by on the current – plankton, fish eggs, minute crustaceans. Hundreds of these eels can be found together, swaying like hosepipes as they feed, creating a bizarre kind of living garden. If danger appears, they slither quickly into the sand. These 'garden eels' can even mate while securely embedded in the sand: the male wraps his body around the female and fertilises the eggs while both remain firmly anchored in their own holes.

COLD SHALLOWS

The extraordinary undersea world of coral reefs has become familiar to us through the work of marine photographers. The warm, clear waters of the tropics offer perfect conditions for such work. Less familiar are the undersea worlds of colder regions. Yet many coastal waters in temperate regions are packed with life – and it is often as rich and as varied as the life around tropical coral reefs.

In shallow waters off the coast of southwestern England, for instance, there are

COLD-WATER CORAL *Soft corals, such as sea fans, can tolerate the cold and the dim light of greater depths.*

spectacular stands of feathery soft coral. Fan worms, jewel anemones with their sparkling arrays of tentacles and cuttlefish add to the

EATING TOOL *Sea otters place stones on their chests to crack open shells – a rare example of animals using a tool.*

open the shells of abalone, clams and urchins against stones that they balance like portable anvils on their chests.

THE DROP OFF

Life becomes more scarce the deeper you go. Off the Cayman Islands the seabed slopes downwards past stands of coral, and then drops away to form the Cayman Wall. It is a dramatic display of how life forms change with depth. After 150 ft (45 m) the coral peters out, but its sculptural shapes are matched by 'soft corals' such as gorgonian sea fans and huge sponges shaped like barrels, vases and strands of rope. Brittle stars, spidery relatives of starfish, with fern-like arms, writhe across the rocks. Large fish, such as groupers, inhabit these depths, as do the sea's top predators: the sharks. The sea begins to darken beyond this, gradually falling out of reach of the sun's illumination. Below lies the vast, dark world of the ocean deeps.

embedded on their base. Amazingly, they do not seem to be harmed by this: most return to normal when the sea warms up.

In certain parts of the ocean, notably in the cool currents off the west coasts of North America, South America and South Africa, giant algae called kelp grow upwards towards the light from their tough 'holdfasts' that grip the seabed. They can grow up to 200 ft (60 m) tall, creating beautiful, gently swaying worlds bathed in a soft green light. The giant kelp (*Macrocystis pyrifera*) is the world's fastest growing plant, capable of adding 2 ft (61 cm) to its length in a day.

These 'kelp forests' are home to some 750 animal species, and there may be as many as half a million animals on a single plant. They include snails such as sea hares, crabs and sea urchins, all of which graze on the kelp. The kelp forests also act as nurseries for the larvae of urchins and sponges;

cuttlefish and horn sharks attach their egg sacs to the fronds. Bright blue-banded gobies and orange Garibaldi fish dart in and out of the cover of the fronds, while bulky sea lions move sleekly through them with remarkable speed considering their size, in pursuit of prey. Sea otters may be seen swimming on their backs at the surface, breaking

NOT SO SOFT *Some soft corals are not so much soft as flexible. The polyps emerge from branch-like stems that are supported by rods of calcium carbonate called spicules.*

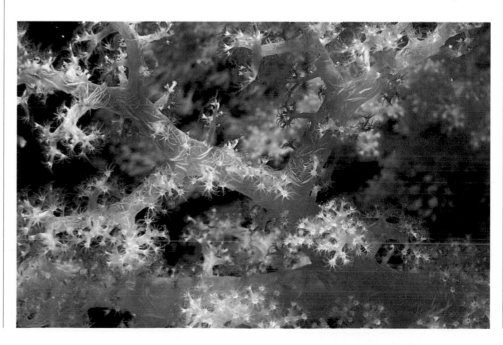

THE OCEAN DEEPS

Some of the strangest creatures on Earth live in the far,

dark depths of the ocean, equipped with fangs and huge

mouths and staring eyes that can spot the glow and flashes

of other creatures moving about in this mysterious world.

Two men peered out of the small, spherical chamber attached to the huge buoyancy tank of their bathyscaphe – a specially built deep-sea research vessel. It was January 1960 and the men were the Swiss oceanographer Jacques Piccard and an American colleague Don Walsh. They had descended to a record depth of 35 810 ft (10 915 m) in the deepest part of the ocean – the Mariana Trench in the north Pacific. Around them, illuminated by a pool of electric light, lay a barren-looking world of grey sediment. Then an extraordinary sight greeted their eyes: a fish – 'A flatfish [at] the very nadir of the earth', as Piccard later put it. Here was evidence that even in this lightless world, packed down under a pressure of 3500 atmospheres, there was life.

More recent exploration in the Mariana Trench, carried out in the 1990s by Japanese robotic submarines, has produced even more remarkable discoveries. Using halogen lamps and cameras sending images to the surface by cable, a desert-like environment of fine, reddish-brown mud was revealed. In the mud of this very still, dark, deep-sea world were tantalising glimpses of a whole variety of creatures never witnessed before – what appeared to be types of sea urchin, marine worm, sea cucumber, jellyfish and crustacean.

ONE AIM *The body of a deep-sea swallower consists of little more than a sack to envelop its prey and the organs to digest it.*

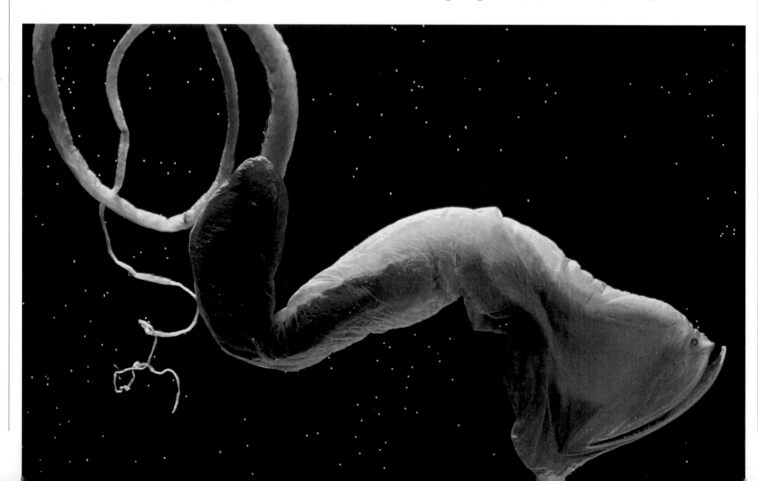

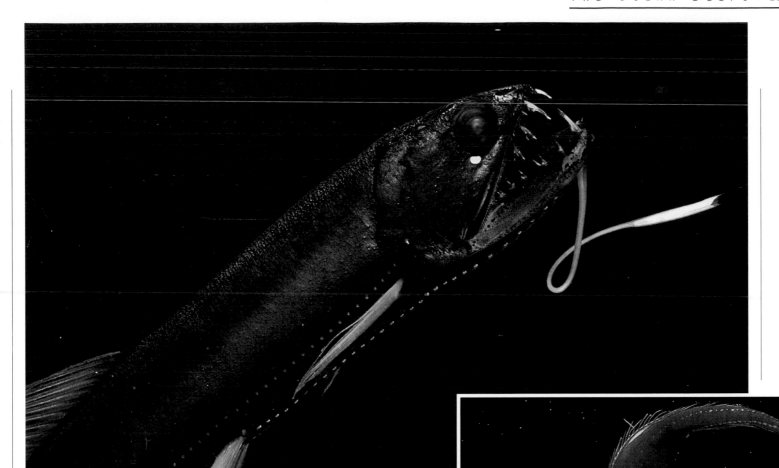

SEARCHLIGHTS *Stomiatoids carry luminescent barbels as lures. Organs below the eye emit red light, so they can spot red creatures that would otherwise be invisible.*

Despite these sightings, the ocean depths are for the most part realms of ghostly emptiness – the very opposite of the teeming life of the coral reefs. At a depth of just 165 ft (50 m) only 5 per cent of sunlight penetrates the sea. Between 1650 ft (500 m) and 3250 ft (1000 m) there is a twilight zone. Beyond that permanent night begins and temperatures drop close to freezing. Because of the lack of light for photosynthesis, no plants can grow below 425 ft (130 m), let alone in the dark depths – except in the nutrient-rich water of rare deep-sea volcanic vents. Even so, about 2000 species of fish and similar numbers of invertebrates have made this shady world their home, feeding on a rain of debris that descends from the life forms higher in the sea, and on each other.

To cope with such conditions, fish have evolved some extraordinary adaptations, all of which conspire to make many of them hideous to our eyes. Success in this vast, dark world depends on being able to make the most of it when it is available. Viperfish have huge curving teeth to clench their prey in a vice-like grip while they swallow it whole; they can also dislocate their jaw, like a snake, in order to consume prey larger than themselves. Some species of fish seem little more than mouths with tails. The black sea dragonfish has a gaping mouth rather like a shopping bag, surrounded by needle-sharp teeth, for scooping up prey; the rest of its body is a small, stalk-like tail. The eel-like fish aptly named gulpers have huge mouths attached to an extendible stomach, which is capable of digesting large fish whole.

Many deep-sea fish, such as the black loosejaw or snake dragonfish, have lights close to their jaws – to lure prey. Several

VACUUMING THE DEEP *Deep-sea gulpers have huge jaws and bag-like stomachs, which enable them to consume prey both large and small.*

have taken this practice one step further by dangling a tempting, glowing bait from the tip of a modified dorsal fin in front of their mouths. The anglers (the females of the species only) are the best known practitioners of this technique, but Sloane's viperfish has a similar appendage. Leaving nothing to chance, the long-fanged viperfish even has lights in the roof of its mouth.

Bioluminescence is not just a matter of attracting prey, however. Many fish – notably

UNDER LIGHTS *Bioluminescent spots on the underside of the hatchet fish deceive potential predators hovering below.*

dragonfish – are speckled with lights that are arranged in patterns and dots along their body. Since male and females often have different sets of lights, biolumines-cence clearly also plays a part in courtship. These lights are presumably one of the rea-sons why many deep-sea fish are equipped with highly sensitive eyes.

Finding mates in a dark and sparsely inhabited world can be difficult. Angler fish have gotten around this in an ingenious way. When the male finds a female he clenches his teeth into her nether region, close to her sex organs. From here he fertilises her eggs – and continues to do so for the rest of his life. Gradually his body merges with hers, degenerating into an appendage which is fed directly from the body of the female.

Just as sperm whales and swordfish occa-sionally drop to depths of 6500 ft (2000 m), so many deep-sea fish come towards the surface at night to feed. Shrimps may make a daily upward journey of 1300 ft (400 m), though many live permanently at depths of

5000 ft (1500 m). Another migrant is the monstrous-looking hatchet fish – not so monstrous when you know that it is only 2½ in (6 cm) long. Hatchet fish are found at depths of 300 ft (90 m) to 1500 ft (450 m). They have an array of blue-green lights along the base of their bodies – a deep-sea example of countershading. Many fish, such as mackerel, have dark upper bodies and lighter undersides, so that from above their colours merge with the sea floor and from below they merge with the light of the sur-face. The hatchet fish has a dark back, but its lights break up the fish's silhouette against the lighter surface of the ocean. Further-more, the hatchet fish seems to be able to regulate the emission of light to match the surrounding conditions.

Most deep-sea creatures escape attention by having dingy, muddy colours, or by being transparent, like jellyfish and glass-sponges. However, various animals living in zones just penetrated by dim light, such as crabs, squid,

LIFE IN THE VENT COMMUNITIES

If the crust of the Earth is divided up into massive tectonic plates, and these are on the move, then lines of stress must occur where the continental plates meet the ocean plates. This was the theory generally held by geologists by the 1970s. Most of these faultlines lie deep beneath the sea. Where they are pulling apart, the scientists reasoned, lava and other volcanic activity should be evident.

It was to test this theory that, during the 1970s, a number of deep-sea expeditions were mounted using a new generation of mini submarine. Fresh lava was found along the Mid-Atlantic Ridge, and in 1977 active volcanic vents were also discovered in the Galápagos Rift, on the East Pacific Rise.

Geologists were delighted with the results – but so were marine biologists, and anyone with an interest in the history of life on Earth. For around the Galápagos vents scientists discovered a range of marine life depending on a life-system never previously encountered.

In the darkness of their deep-sea world, 8500 ft (2600 m) down, the volcanic vents spew out plumes of mineral-rich water at temperatures as high as 350°C (662°F). Bacteria accumulate around the vents, absorbing the minerals, notably hydrogen sulphide, and transforming them into organic matter. This bacteria forms the base of a food chain that feeds unique species of tube worms, and huge clams, and they in turn nourish a variety of fish, crabs, shrimps, even octopus – in other words a whole vent community. Tube worms in particular thrive in these warm, nutrient-rich conditions, reaching lengths of up to 8 ft (2.4 m). Clams grow to 1 ft (30 cm) long.

The animals that gather around the vents are highly specialised; since vents remain active for only a few decades at most, it is a mystery how these specialist species survive the cessation of their vent's activity. But it is possible that sufficient larval forms are present in the surrounding waters to colonise other new vents when they come on stream. Before this discovery, scientists believed that all life on Earth depended on photosynthesis. But there is no light in the depths of the Galápagos Rift: it is the bacteria, feeding off chemicals, that provide the essential foundation for life, in a process called 'chemosynthesis'. It is possible that this phenomenon may not simply be an isolated adaptation, but may have been responsible for producing the very first life on Earth. Bacteria similar to that found on the East Pacific Rise have been identified in rocks at least 3000 million years old. Meanwhile, countless other submarine vents await exploration along the lines of the world's 40 000 miles (64 000 km) of ocean rifts.

BIG CHIMNEYS *Minerals in the magma-heated water solidify to create chimneys, known as 'black smokers'. Bacteria feed on the minerals in the water, supplying the base of the vent community's food chain.*

WILLIAM BEEBE — DISCOVERER OF THE DEEP

During the 1930s the American naturalist William Beebe (1877-1962) became the first person to verify that not only was there life in the deep, but it was richer than anyone had imagined.

It took great courage to achieve this. Beebe's vehicle was a metal ball called a bathysphere, designed by fellow American Otis Barton to withstand the immense pressures of the depths. It was just 4$^{1}/_{2}$ ft (1.4 m) in diameter. Accompanied by Barton and with

six hours' worth of oxygen, Beebe was lowered into the inky blackness at the end of a steel cable. In 1930, working off Bermuda, they reached 1426 ft (434 m), a new record. In 1934, again off Bermuda, they reached 3028 ft (922 m). Throughout the dive, Beebe kept up a running commentary via a telephone link to the surface. This was not only to relay his experiences, but also to signal that all was well. A silence of more than five seconds indicated an emergency.

What Beebe saw through his tiny porthole was an eerie world inhabited by strange-looking luminescent fish of a kind that had only been guessed at from the nets of deep-sea trawlers. He described his experiences in the colourful terms that had made him famous – and which attracted the scorn of the academic world that did not approve

LIFETIME'S STUDY *Beebe was in his fifties, with a celebrated career in zoology behind him, when he made his record dives.*

of the way that he popularised his research. When he described a fish called a Pallid Sailfin as 'bathed in a strange luminosity' his critics claimed that he had been deluded by the lights and thick glass of the bathysphere.

But Beebe was a celebrity, as well as the head of the New York Zoological Department of Tropical Research. He was the author of 23 books and numerous articles, and had a devoted public who lapped up his accounts of field work, whether conducted in the heart of a tropical rain forest or deep beneath the waves.

His 1934 descent in the bathysphere held the record for 15 years. Since then it has been superseded many times over by modern, specially equipped submarines. In 1960 Jacques Piccard and Don Walsh took the bathyscaph *Trieste* ten times deeper, to 35 810 ft (10 915 m), the very bottom of the ocean – but this was a path that Beebe and Barton, dangling in their metal ball from a cable, had helped to pioneer.

MONSTERS OF THE DEEP *Beebe's reports challenged the imagination of illustrators.*

shrimps and starfish are bright red. Colour is reflected light, but water absorbs the colours of the spectrum in a series of gradations. Red is usually absorbed in about the first 25 ft (8 m) of water: thereafter it appears black. Red animals are therefore almost invisible in the shadowy depths.

Species reach monstrous proportions. Sea pens, which grow to a height of 12 in (30 cm) on coral reefs, grow to 8 ft (2.4 m). The body of the giant squid, which lives in depths of up to 8000 ft (2440 m), can reach 12 ft (3.7 m) – but its tentacles, used to catch prey and convey it to its beak, can be more than 40 ft (12 m) long.

RED FOR SAFETY *In the ocean depths red appears black, and so is the colour adopted by many deep-sea creatures, such as this aptly named fangtooth.*

IN ALL ITS GLORY *Squid have especially fine luminescent effects, gliding through the permanent night of the deep sea like illuminated carnival floats.*

Even at depths of 33 000 ft (10 000 m) animals such as sea lilies, anemones, sea cucumbers and bivalve molluscs grow on the seabed, filtering organic material that drifts down from above. Growth at these depths appears to be very slow: some bivalves less than 1 in (2.5 cm) long have been found to be 250 years old. The pressure of the sea increases by one atmosphere every 33 ft (10 m). These animals can cope with the pressures because their bodies contain fluids at the same pressure. If brought to the surface, they explode.

DEEP-SEA VOLCANOES

Deep beneath the surface of the oceans mountain ranges rise in ridges and plunge into deep abysses, covered in the debris of millennia. Many of the ridges mark the lines where faults in the Earth's surface are being pulled asunder. Here volcanic activity spews out clouds of steam, gases and hot magma into the stillness of the deep. With the great pressures of the depths, lava forms globular pillows of basalt, while precipitated minerals such as iron, zinc and copper form chimneys around the vents. Looking like sandcastles

---

THE WORLD'S HIGHEST MOUNTAIN

Mount Everest is the world's highest mountain, rising to 29 028 ft (8848 m) above sea level. But if all the oceans were drained, the statistics would look rather different. Submarine ridges such as the East Pacific Rise are every bit as massive as the great ranges on land. Perhaps the highest mountain in the world should be Mauna Kea in Hawaii. It rises 13 796 ft (4205 m) above sea level, but from the ocean floor it rises some 33 000 ft (10 000 m).

---

made of dribbling sand, some of these can reach heights of 165 ft (50 m) or more. Many of these unearthly features appear as strange excrescences in an empty lunar landscape – but here and there the vents attract prolific outbursts of unique deep-sea life.

These 'vent communities' were first discovered only in the 1970s. Since then scientists have probed further into the ocean depths, using manned mini submarines and robot submarines equipped with cameras and remote-controlled arms. Still, these are mere pinpricks in the vastness of the oceans – and since these expeditions are expensive to mount, progress is slow.

Every now and then the nets of trawlers haul up strange creatures from the depths, such as 'megamouth', a 16 ft (5 m) plankton-eating shark. Only five more have been seen since it was first discovered in 1976 – all males. Another celebrated discovery was the large, scaly fish called a coelacanth, first caught in a trawler's net off South Africa in 1938. Previously known only in fossils, it was believed to have been extinct for 70 million years. Fossils also recorded the vampire squid living 100 million years ago. Now these strange creatures have been found at depths of up to 9000 ft (2750 m). About the size of a hand, their jet-black arms are joined by webs. Such finds remind us that the depths of the ocean remain largely unexplored – and yet from the evidence so far, they rank among the strangest worlds on Earth.

INDEX

PICTURE CREDITS

3 Tom Stack & Associates; 6 OSF/ Richard Parkwood. 7 Robert Harding Picture Library/Pat Gascoigne, TL; 8 DRK Photo/Pat O'Hara, TR. DRK Photo/Kennan Ward, TL. 8-9 NHPA/Martin Harvey. 10 Bruce Coleman Ltd/George Bingham, T; Bruce Coleman Ltd/Stephen J. Doyle, B. 11 NHPA/John Shaw, T; DRK Photo/Larry Ulrich, B. 12 Planet Earth Pictures/Linda Pitkin, T; Tom Stack & Associates/ Randy Morse, B. 13 The Wildlife Collection/Jack Swenson, T; OSF/ Dieter and Mary Plage, B. 14 The Wildlife Collection/Ralph Lee Hopkins. 15 Range/Bettman/UPI, T; NHPA/Kevin Schafer, B. 16 Bruce Coleman Ltd/Luiz Claudio Marigo, T; Siena Artworks Ltd, London/Chris Forsey, B. 17 Ardea London Ltd/ Adrian Warren. 18 Planet Earth Pictures/J.O. Wirminghaus, TL. 18-19 Ardea London Ltd/Ferrero-Labat, B. 19 Bruce Coleman Ltd/Erwin and Peggy Bauer, TL; Planet Earth Pictures/Jonathan Scott, TR; DRK/Stephen Krasemann, B. 20 OSF/Alan and Sandy Carey, TR. 20-21 BIOS/Dominique Halleux. 21 OSF/Survival Anglia/Doug Allan, BR. 22 Robert Harding Picture Library, BL; Comstock Photofile Ltd, BR. 23 DRK Photo/Tom Bean. 24 Range/Bettmann, T; Robert Harding Picture Library, B. 25 DRK Photo/ James P. Rowan, T; Bruce Coleman Ltd/Frances Furlong, B. 26 Bruce Coleman Ltd/Erwin and Peggy Bauer, T; Bruce Coleman Ltd/Hans Reinhard, B. 27 Planet Earth Pictures/Ken Lucas, TL; Planet Earth Pictures/Richard Coomber, TR; Planet Earth Pictures/John Downer, BL; Bruce Coleman Ltd/Dr Eckart Pott, BR. 28 DRK Photo/Larry Ulrich. 29 Bruce Coleman Ltd/Fritz Prenzel, T; The Wildlife Collection/ Neville Coleman, B. 30 Bruce Coleman Ltd, BL; Postojna Caves, Slovenia, BR. 31 Heather Angel, TL; Siena Artworks Ltd, London/Chris Forsey, BR. 32 DRK Photo/C.C. Lockwood, TL; Hedgehog House/ Colin Monteath, BR, BL. 33 Tom Stack & Associates/Harris Photographic. 34-35 Siena Artworks Ltd, London/Chris Forsey. 36 Siena Artworks Ltd, London/Chris Forsey, CL, B; OSF/Clive Bromhall, TR. 37 C.M. Dixon, CR; Range/Bettmann/ UPI, BL. 38-39 Bruce Coleman/ Nicholas de Vore. 39 Siena Artworks Ltd, London/Chris Forsey, T; BIOS/ Peter Weimann, BR. 40 Planet Earth Pictures/Pete Oxford. 41 Ardea London Ltd/ Kenneth W. Fink, TR; Bruce Coleman Ltd/Dr Eckart Pott, B. 42 Bruce Coleman Ltd/Gunther Ziesler, T; The Wildlife Collection/ Henry Holdsworth, B. 43 BIOS/ André Fatras, TL; Bruce Coleman/ Konrad Wothe, TR; Tom Stack & Associates/Larry Lipsky, CR; BIOS/ Cyril Ruoso, BR. 44 Bruce Coleman

Ltd/Gerald Cubitt, T; The Natural History Museum, London, B. 45 OSF/Babs & Bert Wells, TL; Ardea London Ltd/ Jean-Paul Ferrero, BR. 46-47 Robert Harding Picture Library/Geoff Zenner; 47 OSF/ Survival Anglia/Frances Furlong, TR. 48 Bruce Coleman Ltd/Andy Purcell. 49 Planet Earth Pictures/Steve Hopkin, TL; Ardea London Ltd/Liz and Tony Bomford, TR; DRK Photo/ John Gerlach. 50-51 Bruce Coleman Ltd/Andrew J. Purcell. 51 OSF/Harold Taylor, TR; Bruce Coleman Ltd/Waina Cheng Ward, C. 52 BIOS/Marc Rapilliard, TL; Bruce Coleman Ltd/Jane Burton, TR. 53 NHPA/Roger Tidman, T; Tom Stack & Associates/Joanne Lotter, B. 54 NHPA/Anthony Bannister. 55 Siena Artworks Ltd, London/Chris Forsey; Planet Earth Pictures/Jonathan Scott, BR. 56 BIOS/Hubert Klein, B; NHPA/Eric Soper, T. 57 Planet Earth Pictures/J. R. Bracegirdle. 58 DRK Photo/Tom and Pat Leeson, T; Bruce Coleman Ltd/Jeff Foot, B. 59 Planet Earth Pictures/John Eascott/ VVA Momatiuk. 60-61 Siena Artworks Ltd, London/Ron Hayward. 62 Auscape International/Jean-Paul Ferrero. 63 The Wildlife Collection/ Ralph Lee Hopkins, TL; The Wildlife Collection/Martin Harvey, CR; BIOS/Seitre, BR. 64 DRK Photo/ Larry Ulrich; 65 Tom Stack & Associates/Spence Swanger. 66 Tom Stack & Associates/Tom Algire, BL. 66-67 Bruce Coleman Ltd/Jules Cowan, T. 67 Bruce Coleman Ltd/Konrad Wothe, TR. 68 Bruce Coleman Ltd/Dr Eckart Pott, T; OSF/Lon E. Lauber, B. 69 NHPA/ Stephen Dalton, T; Tom Stack & Associates/Mike Bacon, BL; Bruce Coleman Ltd/Rod Williams, BR. 70 Bruce Coleman Ltd/Luiz Claudio Marigo. 71 Planet Earth Pictures/ Richard Matthews, TL; Bruce Coleman Ltd/Hans Reinhard, TR; Bruce Coleman Ltd/Luiz Claudio Marigo, BR. 72 Siena Artworks Ltd, London/Gill Tomblin. 73 DRK Photo/Michael Fogden, CL; DRK Photo/Larry Lipsky. 74 The Wildlife Collection/Charles Gurche. 75 Planet Earth Pictures/Hans Christian Heap, T; Hedgehog House/Tui de Roy, B. 76 BIOS/M. and C. Denis-Huot; 77 DRK Photo/ Michael Fogden. 78 NHPA/A.N.T., TL; Tom Stack & Associates/Rich Buzzelli, BL. 79 OSF/Michael Fogden, TL, TR; NHPA/Christophe Ratier, B. 80 Auscape International/ Hans and Judy Beste, BL; Auscape International/Mike W. Gillam, TR; Bruce Coleman Ltd/Waina Cheng Ward, BR. 81 Bruce Coleman Ltd/ Michael Fogden, TR; NHPA/Stephen Krasemann, BR. 82 Planet Earth Pictures/Alain Dragesco, TL; DRK Photo/Michael Fogden, CR; DRK Photo/Jeff Foot, BR. 83 NHPA/ Anthony Bannister. 84 BIOS/Julien Frebet. 85 Bruce Coleman Ltd/David Houston, B; Bruce Coleman Ltd/Kim Taylor, T. 86 BIOS/Cyril Ruoso, T; Planet Earth Pictures/Lythgoe, B.

87 DRK Photo/Fred Bruemmer, TR; Bruce Coleman Ltd/Dr Charles Henneghien, B. 88 BIOS/Xavier Eichaker, TL; Bruce Coleman Ltd/Atlantide, BR. 89 Bruce Coleman Ltd/ Francisco Futil. 90 NHPA/B. and C. Alexander. 91 OSF/Colin Monteath, TL; DRK Photo/M.C. Chamberlain, TR. 92 Robert Harding Picture Library, TL; Planet Earth Pictures/Philip Sayers, TR. 93 NHPA/B. and C. Alexander, C, TR; BIOS/Hubert Klein, BR. 94 NHPA/John Shaw,TL; OSF/Richard Packwood,BR. 95 Siena Artworks Ltd, London/Chris Forsey, T; Bruce Coleman Ltd/Hans Reinhard, BR. 96 NHPA/Ted Mead. 97 Bruce Coleman Ltd/C.C. Lockwood, TR; Bruce Coleman Ltd/Peter F.R. Jackson, BR. 98 OSF/Dieter and Mary Plage, TL; Robert Harding Picture Library/ Sasson, TR; OSF/Roland Mayr, BR. 99 NHPA/David Woodfall, B; Heather Angel, TR. 100-1 Planet Earth Pictures/Sean Avery. 101 OSF/ Bruce Davidson, T. 102 OSF/Bruce Davidson. 103 DRK Photo/Larry Ulrich. 104 Siena Artworks, London/Chris Forsey. 105 NHPA/ A.N.T., BL; Planet Earth Pictures/Jiri Lochman, BR. 106 Planet Earth Pictures/Wendy Dennis, T; NHPA/B. Jones and M. Shimlock, B. 107 BIOS/ Cyril Ruoso, T; The Wildlife Collection/Henry Holdsworth, B. 108 DRK Photo/Gary Gray. 109 Tom Stack & Associates/John Shaw, TR. 110 DRK Photo/Bob Gurr, BL; DRK Photo/Wayne Lankinen, CR. 111 BIOS/Jean Larivière. 112 Robert Harding Picture Library/Robert Francis, TR; DRK Photo/Annie Griffiths, BL; 113 NHPA/Kevin Schafer, TR; NHPA/Joe Blossom, BR. 114 NHPA/Nigel J Dennis, TL; NHPA/Anthony Bannister, TR. 115 BIOS/Denis-Huot, BL. 116 Tom Stack & Associates/Mary Clay. 117 The Wildlife Collection/Henry Holdsworth, T; DRK Photo/John Eastcott/V.V.A. Momatiuk, B. 118 OSF/N. Rosing/Okapia, BL; BIOS/J.J. Alcalay, TR; 119 DRK Photo/Tom Till, BL; BIOS/William Fautre, TR. 120 Siena Artworks Ltd, London/Sharon McCausland. 121 Tom Stack & Associates/Thomas Kitchen, TR; NHPA/Stephen Krasemann, BR. 122 BIOS/ P. Prokosch/WWF, T; DRK Photo/ Fred Bruemmer, B. 123 Planet Earth Pictures/Seaphot/Georgette Douwma, T; NHPA/Julie Meech, B. 124-5 Bruce Coleman Ltd/David C Houston. 125 Bruce Coleman Ltd/Dr Sandro Prato, TR. 126-7 DRK Photo/ Jeff Foot. 127 BIOS/Brigitte Marcon, TC. 128 Robert Harding Picture Library, T; DRK Photo/D. Cavagnaro, B. 129 Planet Earth Pictures/ Georgette Douwma, T; G.R. Roberts, B. 130 Bruce Coleman Ltd/C.C. Lockwood. 131 NHPA/John Hartley, C; BIOS/Seitre, TR. 132 Robert Harding Picture Library/Maurice Joseph. 133 Robert Harding Picture Library, T, B. 134-5 NHPA/A.N.T. 135 DRK Photo/Michael Fogden, TL;

Planet Earth Pictures/Sean Avery, BR. 136-7 Siena Artworks Ltd, London/Lee Peters. 138 Robert Harding Picture Library, T. 138-9 Planet Earth Pictures/Anup and Mandj Shah, B. 139 DRK Photo/ Barbara Gerlach, TR. 140 Tom Stack & Associates/Randy Morse. 141 Auscape International/Kev Deacon, TR; Auscape International/ L. Newman & A. Flowers, BL. 142 NHPA/Tsuneo Nakamura, TR; NHPA/Kelvin Aitken, B. 143 DRK Photo/Norbert Wu, CL; Planet Earth Pictures/Ken Lucas, TR; NHPA/B. Jones and M. Shimlock, BR. 144 BIOS/Yves Lefevre, TL; Planet Earth Pictures/Gary Bell, BR. 145 Bruce Coleman Ltd/Charles and Sandra Hood, TR; Auscape International/D. Parer & E. Parer-Cook, BL. 146 Planet Earth Pictures/Robert Arnold, T; Planet Earth Pictures/Bill Wood, BR. 147 BIOS/Rafel Al Ma'ary. 148 Tom Stack & Associates/Randy Morse, TL; Planet Earth Pictures/ Georgette Douwma, CB. 149 Siena Artworks Ltd, London/Sharon McCausland, T; Bruce Coleman Ltd/ John Murray, BR. 150 NHPA/ Norbert Wu. 151 Planet Earth Pictures/Peter David, T; NHPA/ Norbert Wu, BR. 152 Planet Earth Pictures/Peter David, T; NHPA/ Norbert Wu, BL. 153 Siena Artworks Ltd, London/Malcolm McGregor. 154 Hulton-Deutsch Collection, TR; Mary Evans Picture Library, CL; Planet Earth Pictures/Norbert Wu, BL. 155 Planet Earth Pictures/Peter David.

FRONT COVER: DRK Photo/ Barbara Gerlach; NHPA/ B. and C. Alexander, C.

BACK COVER: OSF/Richard Packwood.